Impressions of War

The Memoirs of Herbert Hodgson 1893-1974

Edited by Bernard Hodgson and Geoffrey M. Hodgson

Martlet Books

© Bernard Hodgson 2010

First published 2010 by
Martlet Books
8 Withers Close, Oakham, Rutland LE15 6GG
United Kingdom.

All rights reserved. Except for the quotation of short passages for the purposes of criticism and review, no part of this publication may be reproduced, stored in a retrieval system, or transmitted, in any form or by any means, electronic, mechanical, photocopying, recording or otherwise, without the written prior permission of the publisher.

ISBN 978-0-9521853-5-2. Hardcover.

This hardback first edition is printed in a limited run of 300 copies.
This is copy number 230

Printed by CPI Antony Rowe, Chippenham, Wiltshire

Impressions of War

The Memoirs of Herbert Hodgson 1893-1974

Edited by Bernard Hodgson and Geoffrey M. Hodgson

Contents

    Illustrations

    Foreword

1. London Labour and the London Poor   1
2. Called to the Colours   30
3. Pillars of Wisdom   61
4. How Green Was My Valley   83
5. A People at War   112
6. Moving On   124

    Index   135

Illustrations

1. Victoria Platen Press — 16
2. On Brighton Front — 21
3. The Blackfriars Ring about 1900 — 27
4. Bernard Wetherall and Herbert Hodgson about 1912 — 28
5. Rebecca Moore in 1913, Aged 18 — 29
6. Recruiting Poster 1915 — 33
7. Group from the Royal West Surrey Regiment (1) — 35
8. The Northern Sector of the Western Front — 37
9. Group from the Royal West Surrey Regiment (2) — 38
10. Hellfire Corner, Menin Road, near Ypres — 51
11. British Mark I Tank at the Somme, September 1916 — 53
12. Trenches at the Somme, 1916 — 54
13. Herbert and Rebecca Hodgson on their Wedding Day, 1917 — 57
14. W. H. Smith Printing Department in 1922 — 64
15. Lawrence of Arabia at Aqaba, 1917 — 68
16. T. E. Lawrence in 1915 — 75
17. T. E. Lawrence on his Brough Superior Motorcycle, 1927 — 78
18. The Hodgson-Pike 1926 Edition of *The Seven Pillars of Wisdom* — 80
19. Gregynog Hall — 87
20. Main Street, Bettws Cedewain — 90
21. The Venetian Dance Band, circa 1932 — 95
22. A Bombed London Street — 115
23. Street Party, Wedmore Road, Greenford, May 1945 — 123
24. Wedding of Lilian Hodgson and Richard Price, 26 July 1947 — 125
25. Herbert Hodgson and Bernard Wetherall in 1947 — 126
26. Poster for the 1962 Film *Lawrence of Arabia* — 130
27. Herbert Hodgson with his Sons on his 80th Birthday, 2 June 1973 — 133
28. 2008 Gregynog Festival – Books Printed by Herbert Hodgson — 134

Images 1, 3, 6, 10-12, 15, 16-18, 20, 22 and 26 are believed to be out of copyright. Image 28 © Ivor Hodgson 2010. Other illustrations © Bernard Hodgson 2010.

Foreword

Herbert John Robert Hodgson entitled his memoirs *Just an Ordinary Bloke*. But although he came from an ordinary background in South London, he led an extraordinary life. He endured the horrors of the Western Front for four years and survived. His account here of death, heroism and comradeship in the trenches is unique and compelling.

A devoted husband and father, he developed a deep sense of social justice. He greatly enhanced his skills as a printer and by luck these were recognised by several quality presses. That led him to the printing of the extremely rare privately-printed subscribers' edition of T. E. Lawrence's *Seven Pillars of Wisdom* – yet another account of heroism and tragedy in the Great War. This edition is so highly prized for its artwork and Hodgson's printing that single copies fetch up to $80,000 on the market today. Hodgson's account of his meetings with Lawrence is also of historical importance, casting more light on the character of that great enigmatic soldier.

With an established reputation, Hodgson accepted a position for several years at the Gregynog Press in mid-Wales, where contemporary artists Robert Maynard, Horace Bray, Blair Hughes-Stanton and Agnes Miller Parker joined with him. There he helped to create printing masterpieces which will be admired forever. Giants in other spheres of art: Gustav Holst, Sir Adrian Boult, Ralph Vaughan Williams, Sir Henry Walford Davies, George Bernard Shaw and Naomi Mitchison came to marvel at the work produced at Gregynog.

Herbert Hodgson's nine-year period at Gregynog ended in 1936 because of the need to enhance the employment prospects for his growing family. If he hadn't decided to return to London he would have printed more magnificent work at the Gregynog Press.

Little did he anticipate the Second World War and the London Blitz to come, in which he lost one of his sisters. From 1940 to 1952, all his five children served their country in the armed forces. His eldest son fought at El Alamein in 1942 and another served in Palestine after the Second World War.

Impressions of War

Herbert Hodgson was of that unlucky generation, born in the final years of the nineteenth century, who would become deeply involved in the two great global conflicts of the twentieth. Yet he repeatedly referred to himself as a lucky man. No doubt chance played a part, but it cannot account for his extraordinary skill as a printer. In recent years he has been hailed as 'the printer who printed some of the finest twentieth century books.' Another described him as 'as one of the great printers of the twentieth century.' Such numerous testimonials speak for themselves.

His memoirs call not only for social justice, but also for dignity and creative autonomy in the workplace. He was an extraordinary man whose evocative and illuminating memoirs deserve expression in the medium that he mastered.[1]

The editors thank James R. Matheson, Amber Fallow of the New Zealand Press Association, Grahame Armstrong of the *Dominion Post*, the Imperial War Museum, the T. E. Lawrence Society and others for their kind assistance. We are also very grateful for the tremendous support received from members of Herbert Hodgson's family and Jeff Hall for his generosity and reprographic skills.

Bernard Hodgson and Geoffrey M. Hodgson

June 2010

---

[1] Material from chapters 3 and 4 was previously published – in a fine hand-printed edition of 340 copies – as *Herbert Hodgson Printer: Work for T.E. Lawrence and at Gregynog*, Wakefield: Fleece Press, 1989.

We have edited and compressed Hodgson's original text, corrected some errors, removed some repetition and modified the chapter structure. We have added the photographs and – in chapter 4 – extracts from testimonials about his printing work.

Prices in the text are expressed in the pre-decimal coinage of shillings (20 to the pound), guineas (21 shillings), pence (240 to the pound) and farthings (960 to the pound). Some price conversions to current values (using retail price indices) are made in footnotes. All footnotes were added by the editors.

1. London Labour and the London Poor

My father, John George Hodgson, was born in 1859 in Bermondsey, a district adjacent to Camberwell. My mother (Elizabeth Jane, née Skidmore) had first seen the light of day in 1855 in Newgate Street in the City of London. As a printer's labourer living in one of the poorest parts of London, John's main concern was to earn enough money to pay the rent and feed and clothe his growing family. Many of his neighbours were out of work with little or no income.

When I was five, one woman, already worried sick about how to keep her large family from starvation, fell into the depths of despair when another baby, a girl, was born to her. My mother adopted her, bringing her up as one of her own. I knew nothing of this until much later in life and I doubt that the little girl, whose name was Dorothy, was ever adopted officially.

My father worked at a printing works in Shoreditch on the eastern fringe of the City of London. His hours were from 7am to 6pm Monday to Friday and 7am to 4pm on Saturday. His wages were thirty shillings per week and his rent five shillings.[1] He walked five miles to and from work to save the two pennies each way on the trams and buses. On 2 June 1893 I was born in his home at 35 Dragon Road, Camberwell.

The house in Dragon Road was privately owned and one of the then commonplace terraced two-storey houses fronting directly on the street. It had a living room and kitchen downstairs and two bedrooms on the first floor. There was neither gas nor electricity. Lighting was by oil lamps. The only water supply was the cold tap in the kitchen. The kitchen door opened out onto a concrete-paved yard about fifteen by ten feet, some of which was taken up by a small outhouse which contained the toilet. It was an uninviting place with its whitewashed brick walls, high-level cast iron cistern and

---

[1] About £124 and £21 respectively at 2010 prices.

Impressions of War

continual smell. At least it was a modern flush toilet, my father could remember when sanitation consisted of a bucket which was emptied once a week by the 'night-soil' man with his horse and cart. The toilet seat was a plain wooden board and the toilet was back-to-back with that next door.

We didn't have much furniture in the house and what we had was bought second-hand. The living room had a table, four upright chairs, two armchairs and a sideboard. The floor was covered in linoleum, or oilcloth as it was then known, with a few coconut mats dotted about. Some relief was provided by the many pictures hanging on the walls.

There was a cast iron kitchen range in the living room comprising an open fire with an oven on one side and a boiler on the other. We had a bath once a week when the tin bath hanging on a nail in the yard was brought in and placed in front of the fire. My mother would then bale out saucepans-full of hot water from the boiler and we'd be bathed two at a time. Coal for the fire was stored in the yard and when delivered had to be humped through the passage and kitchen.

My parents had a double bed, a tiny washstand and one wardrobe. You could hardly get into the other bedroom where my sisters and I slept. Crammed into it were a double and a single bed and a chest of drawers. I slept in the single bed with my youngest sister Dorothy (called Dolly at home). To get into it we had to climb across the double bed, where my three elder sisters slept: Elizabeth (called Lily at home), Elsie and Kate (born in 1888, 1890 and 1891 respectively).

My mother did her shopping in nearby Walworth and Westmorland Roads where there were shops and market stalls. It was claimed that you could buy anything from 'a mink coat to a rusty nail'. Everything was so unhygienic. On the butchers' stall the unwrapped meat was on open display without any protection and women would pick up chops and joints with their fingers prodding and noses sniffing them over. At dusk oil lanterns were lit on each stall. Saturday was the busiest day and late in the evening the butcher would auction off unsold meat to a large crowd wishing to buy cheap pieces for the Sunday dinner.

London Labour and the London Poor

In many streets there were signs of cottage industry at work. The lady of the house would make and sell toffee apples and other cheap sweetmeats to supplement the family income. In a long street well away from the shops another householder would sell sweets, cigarettes and tobacco at slightly cheaper rates than the shops. In another household the lady would be a seamstress making size changes to garments bought at jumble sales or second-hand clothes shops or to 'hand-me-downs' in the family. Everything was geared to saving money, pennies really. In the shopping parades you would find second-hand furniture and second-hand clothes shops, their ware displayed on the pavement. There would be an oil shop catering for house lamps and a milliner for women who, even in the poorest areas, insisted upon wearing a hat when outdoors. My mother, like thousands like her, took in 'out-work' – sewing buttons on cards. She was helped by my three elder sisters. But I was never asked to help.

There was the muffin man, skilfully balancing on his head a tray full of muffins and crumpets all covered with a white sheet. He rang a large bell with one hand and served his ware with the other, without ever using his hands to steady the tray. I can still taste those muffins buttered after being toasted over the open fire in our living room. The baked-potato man pushed a barrow through the streets, on which was a small coal brazier. Those baked potatoes were not only delicious to eat but great to keep ones hands warm on a cold winter night. The 'cats-meat' man used to come around every week selling, for a penny, six little pieces of horse flesh, between one and two inches square, skewered on a piece of stick. They were all in a basket, arranged in rows. He came down the street like the Pied Piper of Hamelin, but instead of children following him there were hundreds of cats, making one heck of a noise. In summer the 'fly-catcher man' was very popular. He sold rolls of sticky paper covered in gum which would be hung up in every room of the house to catch the thousands of flies which appeared. Food shops were always festooned with flypapers.

Horse-drawn vehicles were abundant and the streets were strewn with droppings. In hot weather the smell could be awful. To bring some colour into their otherwise drab lives people tried to cultivate a

Impressions of War

few flowers in the back yard. The amount of available sunlight was pretty meagre but the horse droppings, carefully gathered in a bucket, helped a little. Some people made barrows out of soap boxes and old pram wheels and sent their kids roaming the streets to collect manure. When another baby was born the barrow would be scrubbed clean with Lifebuoy soap and used as a pram.

The bobby on the beat was a familiar sight. In rough areas they patrolled in pairs and at night each policeman carried a large bullseye lantern. The lamplighter with his long pole would light every lamp in the street. The milkman drove a horse-drawn cart, full of milk churns. He also had one-and-a-half-pint cans which he'd fill with a ladle. He would employ schoolboys to help him on his round, usually between four and five in the morning.

I didn't see much of my father until I was seven or eight years old. For six days of the week he left home in the morning well before I got up and from Monday to Friday he arrived home after I was abed. But he was always there on Saturday evenings and we would all have supper together. One of my sisters, or I when I was old enough, would be sent to the butchers for two-pennyworth of bones and one-pennyworth of pot herbs, the latter consisting of a turnip, a couple of carrots and an onion. Two dumplings would be added and a stew was soon in the making. There wasn't much meat on the bones and one had to use a lot of imagination when eating it. After supper my father would enjoy one of his luxuries – a pint of beer brought from the local pub by my mother or one of my sisters. There was no bottled beer available but every pub had its own 'Jug and Bottle' door where customers took their own receptacle to be filled. There was no restriction on who was served and in time it became my regular job. Often I would meet up with one of my friends on the same beer-fetching errand and neither of us would be able to resist the temptation of having a taste on the way home.

I went to Sunday school with my sisters – a little mission hall in Albany Road. I was frightened by Satan and the blood-curdling things that could happen to naughty children. I remember nothing about the more inspiring side of the Christian faith. Sometimes on a Sunday our parents would take us out, either to a local park or, as a special treat, to see the 'eighth wonder of the world' – Tower Bridge. Seeing the leaves of this bascule bridge being raised was exciting enough, and the sight of the tall ships that passed through into the Pool of London was even more of a thrill.

Often on a Sunday morning my father would take me out for a walk, which usually meant calling at a number of pubs. 'We'll gauge it up, Bert' he'd say, holding up one hand and counting out the names of five pubs on his fingers. We'd stop at each one, where the routine would be the same. He'd go inside leaving me on the pavement. Minutes later he'd reappear and hand me a glass of Sarsaparilla. 'Don't drink it all at once' he'd say, wink at me and go back inside. Sarsaparilla, much prized by youngsters, was really only carbonated water coloured with artificial fruit flavouring. I'd stand outside the pub drinking it, watched with envy by two or three other boys, until my father appeared. I would leave half an inch of drink in the bottom of my glass and hand it magnanimously to the other boys, exhorting them 'not to drink it all at once' and walk off down the street with my father.

By the time I started school my father's employment was intermittent. There was neither dole nor national insurance. How my parents managed I don't know. There were plenty of times when money was so scarce that for breakfast my four sisters and I would be sent to the mission hall in Albany Road. There at 7am we would be served with a slice of currant bread and mug of milk-less cocoa, all for a farthing each. The currant loaves were bigger and longer than ordinary loaves. The smaller children used to be pushed along by the others so that they got the smaller pieces. There we all were, sitting on hard forms munching the dry bread with both hands, pausing now and then to sip the cocoa. You didn't dare put your bread down otherwise it would be quickly snapped up by one of the others. To us it was the feast of the gods. The mission hall was also a soup kitchen where, for a halfpenny, you would be served with a can of soup and a piece of bread. Whole families would eat there. For some it was their only meal of the day. Most youngsters around our way knew what it was like to go to bed hungry. The mission hall was next to R. White's Mineral Water factory and was run by a Mr Roe.

Impressions of War

He went to work each day but must have risen at the crack of dawn to serve us kids. After returning from work he opened the mission in the evenings and weekends.

I remember the patriotic fervour on the outbreak of the Boer War. I understood this as 'boar'. I couldn't understand why everybody was so excited about fighting a lot of pigs. On Saturday mornings one of my jobs was to clean the cutlery. We couldn't afford stainless steel and if it wasn't cleaned weekly it became very discoloured. The knives were cleaned with a piece of emery paper nailed to a board. Forks and spoons were cleaned with Bath brick powder. I was given a second job of shaking out the floor mats from the passage which led to the front door. This meant opening the front door and shaking them out on the pavement. On a windy day most of the dust went straight back in the house. Most boys of my age down our street had the same Saturday morning job and inevitably we would end up throwing the mats at each other until our mothers came out and shouted at us. I remember that the mats got mixed up once and in the panic after being shouted at I took a wrong mat indoors. It was a rather scruffy one. My mother was too proud to go knocking at the neighbour's doors to find ours.

I attended Gloucester Road School in Peckham. There were about sixty of us in one class and it was a heck of a job to keep us in order. The Headmaster was Mr Chase and his staff tried hard. Compulsory education was comparatively new, and there were always plenty of absentees. Some of this was due to parents deliberately keeping their children away from school to do some menial chore or work to help with the family budget. Other children would be kept at home because they had no decent clothes to go out in. I remember we looked an ill-assorted bunch, mostly dressed in second-hand clothes bought from the stalls or in 'cut-me downs' from older children in the family. Mr Chase instituted a Guild of Courtesy at the school. The idea was to act politely to everyone especially ladies and to respect our elders. Most of us qualified for a certificate and badge to wear. Mind you, old Chase was very strict and used his cane a lot. The canings took place in front of the whole class. Any boy who cried was laughed at by all.

London Labour and the London Poor

When I was about ten, Bernard Wetherall and I embarked on our life-long friendship. John Flynn, an Irishman, taught us basic subjects and tried to instil an appreciation of music and drama. He liked Shakespeare and got us to perform *A Midsummer Night's Dream*. I played Puck. Our pronunciation of the prose left a lot to be desired and we couldn't help giggling every time Bottom was mentioned. I was interested in music and Flynn taught me how to read the notation. But when it came to singing I was not very tuneful. Flynn had a little pointed beard which would bob up and down as he conducted with his baton. Anybody who strayed off the note got the baton thrown at him. But he was basically a kindly man.

Most boys belonged to a gang and each gang had an initiation ritual. When I first joined I was told that there was a tree in a park a couple of miles away where, if you put your ear against the trunk, you could hear beautiful music and singing. I went along and all the way there they were saying how wonderful it was. When we arrived each boy put his ear to the trunk and then, with a sigh of ecstasy, raved about the sounds coming from it. 'Come on, Oddy,' they said, 'you have a go.' I couldn't hear a thing and was told to listen harder and press my ear closer. Suddenly one of them gave me a hefty blow on the side of my head. I heard music and singing all right. That got me into the gang. When the next recruit came along I had to do the same to him.

By running an errand for someone, often to the Jug and Bottle or the pawnbroker, we usually had a halfpenny or farthing to spend, and sometimes a whole penny – a fortune to us.[2] Oranges and apples were four a penny and bananas a halfpenny each. There was a sweetshop opposite our school where we could buy 'hundreds and thousands' at one penny for half a pound in weight. It was a sticky mess of small pieces of sweet stuff in all colours.

We used to buy jelly rats and push them along the pencil recesses of the desks to each other until the harassed teacher saw us. His waste-paper basket was always full of confiscated sweets, but when school was finished for the day and he wasn't looking, there would

---

[2] In 2010 prices a penny is equivalent to about £0.32 and a farthing £0.08.

be a fine old scrap over the contents of the basket. We would grab and eat anything that came out.

At the baker's, some bread, buns and cakes were two days old and still fairly fresh; they were sold at three a penny instead of a penny each for those in mint condition. The grocer would sell a bag of broken biscuits for a halfpenny. Many families relied on this cheap fare and very rarely ate fresh produce. My mother bought stale bread to make bread-and-butter puddings and bread puddings. Bakeries were sweat shops. Employees worked a hundred hours a week, stripped to the waist in stifling conditions.

Families were larger then. It was a matter of self-preservation. With enough children you would be looked after in your old age. Even so, there was often the pitiful sight of an old couple being turned out of the family home. The workhouse was the end of the road for the destitute. There was one near us in Westmorland Road – a drab and mournful-looking place. Dressed in shapeless grey uniforms, workhouse inmates would rummage through the market stalls to buy little luxuries with the few pennies they earned working long hours for their keep in the workhouse. Those who couldn't work lived lives of bare subsistence. It wasn't just old people. Whole families, completely destitute and turned out of their lodgings, would end in the workhouse with husbands and wives separated. But I suppose the workhouse system, horrible now to contemplate, was nevertheless a sign of an awakening social conscience. If there had been no workhouses what would people have done? Thrown themselves in the Thames perhaps?

I ran errands to Uncle, as the pawnbroker was known. The favourite item to pawn was father's Sunday suit. Regular as clockwork in some families it would go in on Monday morning and come out on Saturday evening in time for him to look resplendent the next day. One of our neighbours played a large tuba in two brass bands, the Salvation Army and the Army Volunteers (the forerunner of the Territorial Army) and he had two smart uniforms. Every Monday morning his tiny wife would carry his huge tuba in its green baize bag along to Uncle. She kept it secret from her husband until one week she pawned one of his uniforms as well, and didn't have the money to retrieve either on Saturday. They lived a few doors from us but you could hear the row from our kitchen.

Monday was washday. When we came home from school at lunch time our mother would be enveloped in clouds of steam from the boiling copper. We knew what to expect for our meal on those days. She would have made a currant duff or spotted dick as it was known. It was made from a pennyworth of suet, some flour and a few currants, all rolled into a sheet or pillow case, tied at the neck with a piece of string and boiled in a saucepan. Each of us had a chunk and that was our lot until tea-time. Tea consisted of bread and margarine spread with jam, marmalade, treacle or dripping. Sometimes, if there was a bit of extra money in the house, we'd have a bloater or kipper.

Our parents couldn't afford to give us toys, so we had to make up our own games with whatever came to hand. I didn't ride a bike until I was ten years old and then it was an old boneshaker 'borrowed' by one of my friends from his Dad. We all took it in turns to ride it down an incline in the road. I was given a push and away I went. My main concern, never having ridden before, was to keep upright. Near the bottom of the hill were two boys pulling and pushing a cartload of horse manure. I headed straight towards them but they saw me and made an effort to pull the cart across the road. I landed in the middle of it, bike and all. I was sent to bed early that night.

Although strictly forbidden by our parents, we used to play along the Grand Surrey Canal. One evening, walking along a narrow ledge, I fell in. Fortunately it wasn't very deep, just up to my shoulders, but I was soaked. I was pulled out by a bargeman but I was too scared to go home and face my father's belt. One boy suggested that we tell him that I had been riding on the back of the water cart and that the driver had suddenly pulled the lever and I'd got soaked that way. I squelched home feeling very sorry for myself and in some fear and trepidation. I remember my mother saying 'You'd better get those things off and have a hot bath.' She boiled some water and fetched the tin bath from its nail outside the toilet. I jumped in and shot off to bed before my father came home. Later that evening he came into the bedroom and said: 'Have you been down that ruddy canal again?'

'No Dad,' I lied, and told him about the water cart.

Impressions of War

'The carts aren't about in the evening' he replied. 'They only come out in the afternoons to cool the road when the sun is hot.' I had no answer. He simply said: 'You'd better learn to swim.'

After that we used to go to the local swimming baths every Saturday morning. It cost a penny each and we soon learned to take care of ourselves in the water. Strangely, having learned to swim, the canal had no further fascination for us.

There was a little greengrocers' shop near the end of our street. We'd get a length of cotton, a button and a pin. One end of the cotton would be tied to the pin and the button tied about three inches from it. When the greengrocer wasn't looking we'd stick the pin in the frame over his door, leaving the button dangling in front of the glass, then retreat to the street corner holding on to the other end of the cotton. Every now and again a gentle pull on the cotton would set the button tapping on the glass and the poor old greengrocer would have to leave whatever he was doing to see who was at his door. Of course he didn't notice the button or the cotton.

The fronts of the houses were grouped in pairs along the street. Each had a cast-iron door knocker. We'd join two up with a taut length of string, bang on one of the doors and run up the street. The householder would open his door, find no-one there and close it again. The action of opening the door would raise the next door's knocker and closing the door made it clatter. This would bring the neighbour to his door and the farce would be repeated. We would be standing some way off, kicking a ball about, silently doubled up with mirth, especially when it got to the point when they both rumbled what had been happening and were trying to open their doors at the same time. Our gang thought this was far more sophisticated than the simple trick of knocking on somebody's door and running away.

The ball would often be a bundle of rags, tied tightly into a near-round shape. Tops were very popular – a piece of wood shaped like a mushroom with a boot stud hammered into its thin end. Sometimes the top would have a piece of string around it. You then slung the top along the road where it would spin for awhile. There were tops that could be kept going by whipping them along. These weren't so popular with people walking along the pavement or the drivers of horse-drawn vehicles. If you had a whip with a leather thong, the top would go flying up in the air and land anywhere.

There were horse-drawn buses and trams, each with a top deck open to the elements. When the conductor was upstairs we'd steal a ride until he came down and we'd have to jump off; then we'd often fall and get smothered in mud. Electric trams and motorised buses put a stop to that lark: they were a bit too fast. Motor buses gradually replaced the horse-drawn vehicles. For some time you could see both on the streets. The motor buses were not very reliable, always breaking down. When a horse-drawn bus passed a broken down motor bus the horse driver would shout 'Put his nosebag on, mate!'

We could not afford for my Dad to take time off without pay, so my parents never went on holiday. Most employers would have disapproved of any time off. But my parents did manage to contribute one penny per week for each child to the Children's Country Holiday Fund.[3] As long as a family kept up its weekly contribution the children were entitled to a two-week holiday in the country within sixty miles of London. For four years my sisters and I all benefitted. We were separated and went to different places. I remember how excited I used to get the night before I was due to go; sleep was impossible. Packing was easy; we had few clothes anyway. Mine were placed in an old carpet bag and I'd assemble at the mission hall in Albany Road along with other lucky kids. We'd have a destination label pinned to our coats or jerseys, followed by a roll call. Some horse brakes took us to the railway station. The brakes were not like buses. Accommodation for passengers was on the top deck only, accessible up little iron steps. The seats were plain wooden forms and the wheels were also made of wood ringed with iron. The top deck was open to all weathers. The driver sat up front wearing a top hat and with gaily-coloured ribbons on his whip. When we were all seated he gave a flourish of his whip, shouted 'Git up, there' to the pair of horses and away we went, hanging on like grim

---

[3] Established in 1877, the CCHF was set up for poor children by the socialist philanthropist Henrietta Barnett (1851-1936). The charity is still in operation today.

Impressions of War

death and feeling every bump under the wheels. If you overbalanced you fell into the road.

We didn't mind the danger. We were going on holiday and the exhilaration was infectious. We'd shout at people along the streets and any youngster who couldn't come because his parents couldn't afford it had a broadside of: 'Garn, bet you wish you was comin' wiv us.' We'd sing some of the songs we sang at school and I remember how the horses would flatten their ears at the noise. The excitement became greater when we reached one of the London termini. We were going on a train! We'd be marched along the platform to the cheapest seats at the front of the train, be allowed to walk a little way to gaze at the giant engine and then we'd scramble into the compartment and fight for a window seat. After the first puff of the engine starting, we'd be hanging out of the windows watching the clouds of steam and smoke.

The adult with us had no chance of calming us down, nor of keeping the train windows closed. These had heavy wooden frames and were closed by pulling a thick leather strap. We'd pretend it was too heavy. After all, part of the excitement of being on a train was to feel the air rushing in and to smell the smoke. We only got the chance once a year and we weren't going to miss out. Our minder must have been very relieved when the journey was over.

My first holiday destination was Helions Bumpstead in Suffolk. We were met by a bevy of people and paired off, each person taking two children. I was put in the charge of a lady who had a pony and trap and we climbed aboard. What a thrill that ride was. She had a little cottage and kept hens. The contrast with South London was unbelievable. No grimy streets, no dark houses, no back yards. A few pretty cottages, all with gardens, a little church on the hill and open fields all around. And an egg for breakfast every morning! We would go to the henhouse with our hostess and choose our egg.

We'd seen pictures of farms in books and magazines. Now we were taken to a real one. The village blacksmith was a big, hefty, muscular man, a veritable giant to us. Even the horses seemed bigger. And I remember the smell of red-hot metal on the horses' hooves. The days passed quickly, roaming the fields, scrumping apples and pears, bird-nesting, and the village church on Sunday. Smarden in Kent and Farringdon in Berkshire were other places I visited in subsequent years.

Advertising was on walls, hoardings, buses and trams. OXO was priced at a penny a cube, with a picture of a bullock looking at a jar of OXO and saying: 'Alas, my poor brother.' The Bovril advert pictured a sailor floating on a raft in the middle of the ocean with his arms around a bottle of the substance, the caption being: 'Bovril prevents that sinking feeling.' Beecham's Pills were advertised as being 'Worth a guinea a box' and Kruschen Salts had an illustration of a toothless Granddad jumping over a five-barred gate. Cocoa, advertised as being 'good for you', was drunk in abundance. The most famous brand had the slogan 'Sandow's for Strength'. It was named after a strong man who used to appear on the music halls.

First appearing in 1887, a famous advertisement featured the John Millais painting of his little grandson with his golden curly hair, blowing bubbles out of a clay pipe, and with a cake of Pears soap beside him. My mother could afford only cheap carbolic soap. I tried blowing bubbles once with that but the taste in my mouth made me sick. In some families, soap was used only for washing clothes and then not very often. It was an expensive luxury.

I never had pocket money. When I was twelve I got my first job, two evenings a week helping a man who made bushel baskets for Covent Garden – then a centre for trading in fruit, vegetables and flowers. For four hours work I got the princely sum of three pence. As far as I was concerned it was a fortune. I remember blowing my first week's wages in one evening on sweets, fish, pease pudding and chips. My parents scolded me for being so profligate.

The only time when my parents could spend money on non-essential things was at Christmas. The season was nothing like as commercial as it is now, but the practice of hanging up stockings on the bedpost on Christmas Eve was well established. And of course every house had a chimney, which we used to peep up before going to bed and dreaming of what Father Christmas might bring us. In the morning our stockings would contain an orange (a luxury in those days), some sweets and in mine a small wooden train which could be propelled along the floor by hand and my sisters would have a skipping rope each. We were overjoyed.

A few months before Christmas my mother would join a 'goose club', contributing sixpence per week. She would pay in a similar amount at the grocer's so that Christmas Dinner would consist of roast goose and other essentials. What a feast that was! And for about two weeks afterwards we lived on the goose-fat dripping.

To keep our hands warm in winter, we'd find an old tin, pierce a hole in the bottom, thread a piece of string through it, fill the tin with old rags and then set them alight. The rags would then smoulder and by whirling the tin round and round with the string it would heat up for us to wrap our hands around.

I wasn't sorry when I left school in 1907. My teachers had tried hard with me but my academic progress had been slow. Anyway I could read, write and do simple arithmetic. I remember lining up with the other children of the same age to say goodbye to Mr Chase our headmaster. He asked each in turn whether they had a job. I was one of the few who said yes and was able to tell him that I was going to be a printer like my father and that my dad had arranged for me to become an apprentice at his place of work.

My dad's firm was located in the City of London near Ludgate Hill. My hours were 8am to 7pm, Monday to Friday, and 8am to 1pm on Saturdays. To be in on time I had to leave our house in Peckham at 6.30am, catch a tram to the Elephant and Castle, another to London Bridge and a bus to St Paul's.

But the great compensation was the money in my pocket, not that there was much left over after I had paid my fares and given my mum something towards my keep. In my first year my wages were seven shillings and sixpence for a fifty-six hour week.[4] I cut my fares down to two shillings a week by walking each way between London Bridge and work. I gave my mum half-a-crown and I had three shillings for myself.

My sisters Lily and Kate were away in domestic service and Elsie worked in a local factory. When my younger sister Dolly left school

---

[4] Equivalent to about £30 a week in 2010 prices

five years after me she followed Elsie into factory work. With Lily and Kate away, Elsie and I contributing towards the family budget, and my father in regular work, we were one of the lucky families. Saturday night supper was no longer stew made from scrag-ends of meat and we had a roast on Sundays.

My father became a machine minder and I was to learn the trade of printing. Young apprentices were known as 'printers devils' and the apprenticeship period was seven years. In the first year I didn't learn a lot about printing but I became an expert in odd jobs, one of which was to pop out to the nearest Jug and Bottle every morning. The beer was the morning refreshment for the machine minders. They would have been insulted if someone had offered them tea.

Another errand was to go to a factory in City Road and buy sticks of *gutta percha*, a black substance made from the *percha* trees of Malaysia. Heated it melted like sealing wax and was used to stick lead, cork or card in various places on the machine when printing. Snuff taking was prevalent in those days, particularly among compositors and regular trips to the tobacconist also became part of my routine. The printing type used was made from lead which was made in a foundry; the type cases always contained quite a lot of dangerous lead dust. The snuff-taking cleared the nose and throat and helped to prevent lead poisoning. Later all the type was machine made and there was less dust.

Printing was on non-automatic machines where the paper had to be hand-fed. Automatic machines had been invented but were used for printing newspapers only. Our machines were driven by a gas engine and getting it started in the morning was a devil of a job. The engine would be lit and four men would get hold of the big fly-wheel and pull it back in reverse. Once released, and with a bit of luck, the engine would start. In a cacophony of sound, the print machines would spring into life, each one driven by a belt attached to a common drive shaft. Then the machine minders would be hard at it. Occasionally there would be a shout as a drive belt broke and all the machines would have to stop as the belt was repaired. Sometimes a broken belt swirled round and hit the minder. I saw many nasty injuries in those first few years before the installation of protective cases around the belts.

Victoria Platen Press

We had also a hand-fed Victoria platen machine.[5] The machine stood against a brick wall and the man who operated it was sixty-five years of age. He had started work in the firm at the age of twelve and once he had learned how to operate that machine at about sixteen he had sat in the same position facing the characterless brick wall operating the platen machine all of that time. He had 'platen minders finger'. After placing the paper on the platen you are supposed to put the guard in position before letting the platen go up. Familiarity breeds over-confidence, and platen minders come to look upon the guard as an encumbrance. They stop using it, and one day fail to

---

[5] The platen is a flat metal plate that presses the paper against the inked type. By contrast, with a cylinder press, the cylinder holds the paper and rolls over the type. The Victoria platen press was widely used in fine and art printing because of its rigid construction and great printing pressure.

withdraw their fingers in time. The result is a missing tip or more. It had already happened to my father and despite all the warnings it eventually happened to me. It was very painful.

One evening a week I attended the London School of Printing in Blackfriars. I became interested in the history of printing and learned of Gutenberg the German who invented movable type. One of his followers was William Caxton who introduced printing to Britain.

My father printed labels for sticking on the cartons of cylindrical records for the Edison Bell Recording Company, which was based in Peckham, not far from our house. I was given the job of 'gold-dusting' each piece of printed paper as it came off the machine. Actually it was bronze powder-dust and I had to dip into it with some cotton wool and then spread it evenly over the print. I soon got clouds of dust all over me and everything else in sight. There was neither an extraction system nor proper washing facilities. I did that job for some time and travelled home on the tram each night looking like a little golden boy (being called 'Goldilocks' by the conductors), although I only had two pence in my pocket.

The afternoon and evening editions of the papers were delivered by cyclists carrying large canvas bags across their shoulders. Filled with newspapers those bags must have been pretty heavy, but they used to speed along, weaving in and out of the traffic. The batch of papers would be slung across the pavement to street newsvendors.

Crossing the street at a busy junction could be a hazardous business. You could choose between running across between the teams of horses or waiting until there was a traffic jam. Motor vehicles stop still, but horses don't. You were looking out for the traffic rather than to the ground. So by the time you had crossed your boots would be covered in manure. Some enterprising individuals made quite a good living with a bucket of water and a piece of rag cleaning the muck off the boots of city gents at each corner.

The clip-clop of horses' shoes provided a rhythmic accompaniment to the musical sound of their bells. Their harnesses glinting in the sunlight and the coloured ribbons of the driver's whips added to the gaiety. The sounds and colour remained in the winter but the drivers would be huddled up in the cold. Some lucky ones worked for companies that provided greatcoats, but most were wrapped up in sacks in cold and wet weather.

It was always a thrill to see a fire engine pulled by a pair of greys racing to a fire. The horses were so trained that as soon as the alarm bell went in the station they would push themselves out of their stalls and run to either side of the poles of the cart. The driver pulled a cord and the reins fell over the horses' backs. The firemen coupled up the other traces to the fire engine, jumped on and away they all went. It was claimed that it took less than a minute. The horses and fire engines were supplied by Thomas Tilling of Peckham.[6]

Whilst on an errand once I saw three fire engines racing abreast over Blackfriars Bridge. The sparks from the engines and the horses' shoes, the drivers shouting and flailing their whips and the firemen hanging on like grim death was a never-to-be-forgotten sight. I remember being told that the horses were retired after two years of service and that the last horse-drawn service operated from Kensington Gardens. There was a final ceremony when the horses were given carrots and pieces of sugar served on a silver tray.

By the time I got home and had a meal there wasn't time to do very much. I had to be up before six o'clock. Entertainment in the house consisted of listening to my parents discussing the latest gossip along the street. Such talk was always about the more tragic side of life, such as a family who had been evicted from their house for not paying the rent and who had trundled their few pitiful belongings away in a handcart, or of a wife who had been beaten unmercifully by her husband, or of the death of some youngster.

Radios were not yet manufactured and we couldn't afford a gramophone. I joined the local library. I read Fenimore Cooper, R. M. Ballantyne and many more. I bought the weekly boy's

---

[6] Thomas Tilling Ltd was founded in 1846. Its horse buses stopped at predetermined points and ran to a fixed timetable, making them more punctual and reliable than the other operators' buses. By the 1890s Tilling Ltd ran a stable of over four thousand horses in London. After introducing motor buses, the company grew to control almost all the major bus operators in the United Kingdom until nationalization in 1948.

magazines, *The Gem, Buffalo Bill, Boys' Realm* and *Union Jack*. I enjoyed the stories about Billy Bunter, Harry Wharton, Bob Cherry and the rest at Greyfriars, without really understanding what life in a public school was all about. 'What's a quad?' I asked myself. *Union Jack* featured the famous detective Sexton Blake. Again I enjoyed the stories but couldn't help wondering how Blake's parents had come to name him Sexton. I had the same trouble with Sherlock Holmes. I knew of no-one in Peckham called Sexton or Sherlock.

We read Baden-Powell's *Scouting for Boys*. The newly-formed Scout movement offered a variety of interests. The uniforms convinced us: we had never seen their like before. Bernard Wetherall, Ted Smith, I and a few others joined the Scouts and became the nucleus of the first Scout troop in South London. I remember taking part in the first major Scout Rally at the Crystal Palace, where Baden-Powell took the salute.[7]

Scouting took us away from Peckham and I began to appreciate that the countryside was nearer to home than I'd imagined. One weekend Mr Woodgate our Scoutmaster took us on a hike to Sevenoaks in Kent, seventeen miles from our headquarters in Peckham. We got as far as Bromley before several of the younger members dropped out and were sent home by bus or train. By the time we got through Farnborough we numbered five plus the Scoutmaster. Then a blister developed on my foot and I had to pack up. It was about eleven in the evening and I wanted them to leave me. We had camping gear and I said I'd look after myself for the night and get a train back in the morning. The Scoutmaster wouldn't hear of it. He told the others to stay with me and all find our way back in the morning while he pressed on to see if he could complete the hike and reach Sevenoaks. We were all feeling more than a bit

---

[7] Robert Baden-Powell (1857-1941) was a lieutenant-general in the British Army. In the Boer War in 1899 he successfully defended besieged Mafeking. He founded the Boy Scout movement in 1907 and his *Scouting for Boys* was first published in book form in 1908. The 1909 Crystal Palace rally was attended by 11,000 Scouts and was a major launch-pad for the movement.

Impressions of War

tired. I don't think any of us would have made it to the end and there were no objections to his suggestion. We limped back into Farnborough the next morning and got on the first available train.

But the Scoutmaster did not return. We had last seen him trudging off in the darkness with his dog. After a week his family notified the police and we were all interviewed. The police organised a search and the local press carried a story about 'The Missing Scoutmaster'.

His dog was found near Farnborough and returned to his family. That gave us the idea of searching for Mr Woodgate ourselves. We liked the chap and felt responsible. His mother agreed that we should take the dog and gave us some food to take with us. We felt like real detectives. We travelled to Farnborough, walked into the open countryside and searched every field, hedge and pond. We kept it up all day without success and returned home, very disappointed. Later the Scoutmaster turned up, having suffered a loss of memory. A few years later I was to meet him again in very different circumstances.

That experience put us off Scouting. When aged sixteen, Bernard, Ted and I joined the Church Lads' Brigade.[8] We met in a church hall in Peckham Grove and practiced arms drill with wooden rifles.

Army regiments had ceremonial walking-out dress and the chaps coming home on furlough really did look smart with their gold braid. The cavalry and artillery men in striped tight trousers and spurs caught my eye. Most of them had joined up simply to escape the drudgery and degradation of unemployment. All they got was a shilling a day and their keep, but life in a regiment could be tough and hard. I decided that being a printer, though not as glamorous, was more to my liking.

Cycling became a craze at the beginning of the century. We couldn't afford new bikes but there were plenty of second hand ones available. I got a bargain for seven shillings. Other lads bought similar machines and we spent weekends exploring south London and the country beyond. We pedalled as fast as we could but our brakes weren't that good. Electric trams were our biggest headache.

---

[8] The Church Lads' Brigade was founded in London in 1891 by Walter Mallock Gee as a youth group under the direction of the Church of England.

They couldn't deviate from the tracks and to sense one of them bearing down on you from behind was frightening. If we got a wheel of the bike into a tramline in wet weather it always meant a tumble in the road. Trams stopped in the middle of the road and passengers had to cross to the pavement. We sent many a batch of alighting passengers running for cover.

On Brighton Front

Taken 1911 or 1912, Herbert Hodgson is at the front, Bernard Wetherall left rear, and Ted Smith centre rear

When one of us suggested that we try riding to Brighton we all agreed. It was chancy embarking on a 90 mile round trip on unreliable machines. We all worked on Saturdays and so we decided

Impressions of War

to set off on Saturday evening, ride through the night, spend most of Sunday in Brighton and come back on Sunday evening. Our bikes had feeble oil lamps and the streets of south London were not well lit, so it was as well to cover as many miles as we could before darkness fell. The roads beyond London were not very busy; with an occasional motor car and motor cycle.

By ten o'clock we were somewhere south of Crawley. A few miles further we stopped for a rest and something to eat. Using our Scout training we kindled a fire at the side of the road. Our undercooked sausages and unbuttered bread and jam were declared a sumptuous meal. We pressed on to reach Brighton at about three in the morning. We parked our bikes on the sea front, scrambled over the pebbled beach, and stood at the water's edge, peering out into the inky darkness. We were seventeen years of age and it was our first glimpse of the sea.

There were some boats drawn up on the beach. We slipped under the tarpaulins and made ourselves as comfortable as we could. The rushing of the waves was a sound I'd never heard before and I remember dreaming of waking up and finding the boat far out to sea. In fact the boatman stripped back his tarpaulin at about seven o'clock, cursed me roundly, ordered me out of the boat and gave me a wallop as I clambered over the side.

We had about four shillings between us which was enough to see four lads through a day in Brighton. A fish and chip meal was only two old pence. There were some bathers there in their long costumes.

We set off for home at about four o'clock. It started to rain. We had no macs or capes so we sheltered for a while. But we had to press on because we all had jobs to go to on Monday morning. We all got a good soaking. Our machines got us home about midnight. We declared the venture a great success and over the next few years we did the journey four more times. I kept my bike for five years, renovated it and sold it for twelve shillings and sixpence.

I was told at Sunday school that variety theatres were dens of iniquity. I didn't know what that meant but I guessed it wasn't complimentary. Later my eldest sister Elizabeth joined the Salvation Army. Variety theatres and pubs were definitely unpopular with her.

I fell in love with the atmosphere of music halls. My first experience was at about sixteen when my parents took me to Collins' Music Hall in Islington. On the bill that night were Vesta Tilley, Harry Lauder and Eugene Stratton. Vesta Tilley was a male impersonator and considered very daring, dressing up in men's clothes. That night she sang 'I'm following in father's footsteps; I'm following me dear old Dad'. Harry Lauder sang 'Stop your tickling, Jock' and 'I Love a Lassie'. Eugene Stratton, with his face blackened and wearing white gloves, was known as the 'coon singer'. He brought the house down when he sang 'Lily of Laguna', 'I may be crazy but I love you' and 'Little Dolly Daydream'. Even more popular was G. H. Elliot, who also blacked up and called himself the 'chocolate-coloured coon'.[9]

The music hall was pure escapism. Some performances were not very good. Part of the fun was to hiss and cat-call, even to throw rotten vegetables at any turn which didn't impress and keep up the barrage until the performer exited from the stage. Theatre-goers had long memories. A year later someone would appear again but under another name and perhaps with a totally different act. He or she would be instantly recognised and the howl would go up without waiting to see if the act had improved – again a sad exit. I never heard of anyone trying it for a third time.

Every Saturday night Bernard Wetherall and I went to one of the variety theatres. The entrance fee was three pence on Saturdays and two pence on weeknights. We sat in the 'gods', where the excitement was. The vegetable-throwing and cat-calling would start there. Often a fight broke out and the hefty 'chuckers-out' would spring into action. I have since wondered how those old music hall performers made themselves heard above all the noise, yet they did. There were no microphones: they sang, recited or told jokes, totally unamplified.

The shows gave us a chance to hear new songs. Bernard was a gifted pianist and I bought and learned to play an Italian bowl-shaped

---

[9] Of course, such a term would be disapproved of today as an ethnic slur. White singers 'blacking up' remained commonplace entertainment until the demise of BBC Television's 'Black and White Minstrel Show' in 1978.

mandolin. Together with a couple of other lads we formed a musical group and were in great demand at parties and weddings. We were asked to play songs that someone had heard at some theatre and we liked to oblige. As soon as we heard a new song there would be a trip to Chappell's in the West End to buy a sixpenny copy of the sheet music.[10] This contained not only the piano score and mandolin chords but the words for our singers. The wedding receptions we attended were invariably held in the home of the bride's parents. The tiny house would be packed and on summer days would overflow into the street and back yard. The centre of affairs would be the front room or parlour where, if the family could afford it, stood the piano.

The tradition of family entertainment was long established and each member of the family and the guests were also invited to perform. There was never a dull moment. Grandpa would recite 'The Charge of the Light Brigade'. Father would sing 'All that glitters is not gold' – never having seen real gold in his life. Mother would sing 'Two little girls in blue' and Grandma, with tears in her eyes and a cup of gin in her hand, would render an old love song such as 'Old love letters' or 'All that I ask is love'. We would play the hits of the day: 'Nellie Dean', 'Dear Louise', 'If those lips could only speak', 'Thora', 'Lily of Laguna', and 'Just like the ivy on the old garden wall'. The drink was pretty strong and soon the guests would sing loudly. Several would finish up under the table or lying on the stairs, to be carried home later. I remember one wedding where there weren't enough chairs to go round and about six drunken men were sitting on a form. One end collapsed and they fell on top of each other in a heap, out to the world. They stayed there under everybody's feet until the party ended.

We still couldn't resist a practical joke. Ted Smith worked in an engineering firm and brought home some iron filings. Mixed with hydrochloric acid and flowers of sulphur they made wonderfully pungent 'stink bombs' that we put to good use. Once we were on the Embankment at Blackfriars amongst a great crowd of people who

---

[10] Chappell of Bond Street, the historic sheet music and instrument retailer, remains in business today.

had come to see Ernest Shackleton's ship *Nimrod*, which had just returned from Antarctica.[11] One of the lads decided to let them all have a whiff of our 'scent' so he opened the bottle intending to re-cork it quickly. But there was so much jostling going on that the bottle was knocked out of his hand and it smashed on the pavement. I've never seen a crowd melt away so quickly. The sailors on the *Nimrod* must have been amazed. One moment they were being cheered to the echo and the next minute the crowd was in full flight with their faces covered by neckerchiefs, scarves and handkerchiefs. We decided to make ourselves scarce before the law appeared.

The old eating establishments, or coffee shops as they were oddly called, were pretty dingy places in our part of the world. A few marble-topped tables covered with the remains of previous meals or the smear of a dishcloth, some spindly-legged chairs with cane seats, a lino-covered floor from which the pattern had long disappeared and a counter almost entirely taken up with a huge tea urn. But they were cheap. A mug of tea cost a halfpenny and for a penny you could get a cheesecake or a slab of indigestible cake with pink icing on the top. A thick-cut piece of bread and margarine cost a penny and you could have a cooked meal of meat pudding and two veg for four pence or sixpence depending on the size of the meat pudding.

Slightly up-market were 'Pearce and Plenty' dining rooms, which had distorting mirrors either side of the entrance.[12] Customers were

---

[11] Hodgson's draft has 'Captain Scott' rather than Shackleton. But *Nimrod* was Sir Ernest Shackleton's ship; a picture shows it moored at the Embankment in 1909; and no record has been found of such a mooring for Scott's much larger *Discovery*. The expedition of 1907-1909 was the first of Shackleton's three journeys to Antarctica. He reached closer to the South Pole than anyone before and returned home a hero. After running aground on sands off the Norfolk coast in January 1919, *Nimrod* was battered to pieces by a storm. Only two of her crew of twelve survived.

[12] Growing numbers of Londoners travelled such distances to work that it became impossible for them to return home for a midday meal. This led to a big increase in catering facilities, and dining room chains began to be established. Out of the temperance catering movement grew two London

Impressions of War

asked to look at the left-hand one when entering. This depicted them as thin and half-starved with a caption reading 'Before entering'. On the way out they looked in the other and saw a figure resembling Henry the Eighth or Falstaff and read the legend 'Afterwards'.

A building stood on Blackfriars Road that became known as the Ring. Originally built as a chapel, it was circular in shape. It was derelict when taken over by Dick Burge, a well-known boxer and promoter.[13] A number of famous fighters of the day appeared there, including 'Bombardier' Billy Wells, Pat O'Keefe, 'Gunner' Morris and 'Kid' Lewis. I can remember seeing horse-drawn cabs draw up outside the place, bringing 'swells' from the West End and National Sporting Club. There were jugglers, acrobats, fire-eaters, musicians, singers and one-man bands, all scrambling for the odd penny thrown at them. A colourful sight, but symptomatic of a society that was very clearly divided between the haves and have-nots.

At least I was learning a trade and by the time I was eighteen in 1911 things were picking up. Compulsory education had instigated an enormous demand for written matter and newspapers and periodicals were appearing regularly. The 'toiling masses' could now read. Nevertheless poverty could still be seen all around.

---

firms whose main business was providing standardized midday meals of limited variety. Lockharts operated fifty coffee rooms by 1893, while Pearce and Plenty ran twenty dining rooms with the motto: 'Quality, Economy, Despatch.' These were the fast-food outlets of the time.

[13] The Surrey Chapel was built in 1782 for the use of Reverend Rowland Hill (1744-1833), who commissioned the circular design 'for it prevented the devil hiding in any of the corners.' By 1876 the building was used only for illegal cockfighting, which eventually led to its closure in 1881. Bella Burge and her husband, the ex-prize-fighter Dick Burge, acquired the lease for the Surrey Chapel, believing it would make an ideal boxing ring. Their project had been delayed for some years due to Dick Burge's unforeseen incarceration for large-scale fraud. From 1910 it was the notorious Blackfriars Ring, London's premier boxing arena, until it was destroyed in the Blitz. A plaque marks its former position. A pub across the road is called *The Ring* and has pictures of former boxing greats on its walls.

London Labour and the London Poor

The Blackfriars Ring about 1900

I became interested in politics. The message being spread by Keir Hardie and the newly-formed Labour Party appealed to me.[14] But my interest was passive. I couldn't imagine myself being a tub-thumping socialist but I did resolve to vote Labour when I was old enough.

But my friends and I had discovered girls and they were far more exciting than politics. No more cycling or swimming together and we considered ourselves much too adult to be seen in Church Lads' Brigade uniforms anymore. Bernard and I treated ourselves to new suits from a shop in the Walworth Road – Edwardian high-buttoned single-breasted jackets, waistcoats and tight trousers. Straw 'boaters' topped us off and we considered ourselves a couple of dandies. All we needed were girls on our arms. Mine was Rebecca Moore and she lived at 42 Marcia Road just off the Old Kent Road. She was one of

---

[14] The Labour Representation Committee was formed in 1900 and was renamed the Labour Party in 1906. James Keir Hardie (1856-1915) was its leader until 1908.

Impressions of War

Bernard Wetherall (L) **and Herbert Hodgson** (R) **about 1912**

four children with an elder brother and sister and a younger brother. Within a short time of meeting her she became the most beautiful girl in the world to me – my first and only love.

Like so many girls, Becky had no opportunity to study for a career. She worked in Lazenby's (later Crosse and Blackwell's) pickle factory in Bermondsey, wearing a coarse leather apron and clogs, sorting and pickling onions from barrels into jars, ankle deep in vinegar and all for seven shillings a week.

Rebecca Moore in 1913, Aged 18

Marie was Bernard Wetherall's girlfriend and the four of us became firm friends. We hadn't a care in the world. The bioscope cinema one night of the week – showing scratched, grainy, silent films – admission for sixpence each. Perhaps a music hall on a Saturday. No sitting in the 'gods' anymore, we had pit stalls at one shilling each and a box of chocolates (for eight pence) to pass around. Happy courtship days from 1912 to 1914: they passed so quickly and yet the days between meetings seemed so long. Becky was welcomed into my family as I seemed to be with hers. We began to talk of marriage.

1. Called to the Colours

In early 1914 I was twenty years of age and nearing the end of my apprenticeship. I was still at the same firm in Ludgate Circus and had made good progress. I had been turning out work that I considered as good as that turned out by men twice and three times my age. It irked me that they were earning the full rate of two pounds ten shillings a week whilst I was getting only two pounds. I began to question why the apprenticeship had to be as long as seven years. I remember being told by one militant chap that it was the fault of the employers. By keeping the apprenticeship to seven years they obtained a journeyman's work without having to pay the full wage.

One day I discussed it with my father. 'Look,' he said 'supposing the apprenticeship period was cut to say five years, what effect do you think that would have? You realise that apprenticeships in all trades are seven years and you know the reason for that? It is considered the time necessary for a lad to learn everything he should know and it would be against our interests to shorten the period.' I hadn't expected such a response but there was no point in arguing.

New automatic methods of printing were being introduced, particularly for turning out mass-produced commercial work, and the need for finely-honed skills, learned over a seven-year period, was gradually diminishing. I didn't realise this at the time. I had a lurking suspicion that it was all part of a plot to grind us down.

In early 1914 there was talk of war but no-one thought it would come. We became very anti-German – the Kaiser our arch enemy. I had never got rid of my fascination for the army, its glamorous uniforms and marching and parading in the streets. The Territorials paraded on Saturday evenings: they were recruiting drives. While Bernard and I were walking out with our girlfriends one Saturday evening, I voiced what was in our minds: 'I wouldn't mind joining that lot.'

'Nor would I,' said Bernard.

Called to the Colours

'And what would we do on Saturday nights?' retorted the girls.

We appealed to their patriotism and explained that it was our duty. Forebodings of hostilities were rife and we had to do something. After all, the Territorials had been formed for home defence. They accepted this but I'm sure they guessed that there was no stopping us.

In April 1914 I joined the Territorials together with Bernard Wetherall and Ted Smith. At last a uniform to wear, not quite the colourful outfits of the regular army but we felt ten feet tall in our ill-fitting khaki, with puttees and caps. Best of all was the opportunity of weekend camps in the country and an annual fortnight camp during which we received army pay and wages from our employers.

Bernard, Ted and I were signed up by a sergeant major who was a veteran of the Boer War. He was dressed in the normal khaki tunic and trousers but instead of a peaked cap he wore a bush hat, wide-brimmed with one side turned up. We asked if we would be issued with them. He nearly exploded. 'Get some bloody service in before you ask things like that,' he roared. 'Now go in there and get kitted out.' There was a great pile of what turned out to be second-hand Boer War uniforms on the floor of the drill hall. Some recruits were already picking them over. 'Discard any wiv bullet 'oles in 'em' said the sergeant and for a while we took him seriously. We concentrated on the caps to start with.

We were standing there preening ourselves in front of a cracked mirror, caps perched jauntily on our heads, when the sergeant came in again. 'What is this, a bloody mannequin parade?' he thundered. 'Get some bloody uniforms on!' It was the first time I'd seen an angry sergeant major. We found some tunics and trousers which equated roughly to our sizes and lined up in front of him. 'If you weren't so bloody pitiful I'd burst out laughing,' he said, 'and to think that England might have to depend on you lot.' This wasn't quite what we'd expected. The sergeant's acid tongue cast some doubt in our minds that we'd done the right thing.

Towards the end of that evening, during which our Church Lads' Brigade training in drilling had gone some way to persuading him that we might make soldiers after all, the sergeant become quite

Impressions of War

human. We learned that he was seeing out his time, having done twenty years of the twenty one for which he'd signed on.

Before we left, Ted Smith asked him if we could have another look into the pile of uniforms. We'd been told that we were in the 1/24th (County of London) Battalion of the Royal West Surrey Regiment (The Queen's). 'We won't be much of an advertisement for the Regiment, walking down the street like this,' said Ted, indicating the looseness of the uniform hanging around his thin frame. The sergeant relented and we found uniforms that fitted us reasonably well. 'Walk like men when you're wearing the King's uniform,' were the sergeant's parting words.

We didn't just walk; we were so proud we marched. And those Saturday night parades! Marching along to the beat of a drum and fife band, arms swinging and heads held high but eyes swivelling in every direction, imagining that everyone who watched us was filled with admiration! Perhaps they were, patriotic fervour being as it was. But we weren't half as impressive as the regular soldiers.

About a month after we'd enlisted we were told that there would be a two-week camp on Salisbury Plain in August. I hadn't been away for a holiday since the trips to the country in my schooldays. On 5th August we were due to go to camp. We all mustered at our headquarters in Kennington and then marched to Waterloo, where we fell out, awaiting our train. Suddenly a dispatch rider came hurtling into the station on his motor bike. He dismounted and presented an envelope to our commanding officer. The CO opened it, read the contents and gave the order for us to fall in again. 'I have to inform you' he said, 'that the summer camp is cancelled. Great Britain is now at war with Germany.' We marched back to Kennington and were reminded that as Territorials we were now being 'called to the colours' for as long as hostilities lasted. We were to go home for a week, tell our families and employers and then report to Kennington. We were all greatly excited and of course couldn't wait to get home and then back again. The Kaiser was the villain and we were going to show him! People talked about the war being over in a fortnight. There was no conscription. The British army regulars would soon polish off the Germans. All we Territorials had to do was man the home defences, against what we weren't too clear. We returned a week later to be told we were going to St Albans for training and that we would have to march all the way.

Recruiting Poster 1915

We set off jauntily enough, shouting at passers-by and singing and whistling but after a few miles we became a little grim-faced about it. It was a great relief to us to be told that we'd camp at Edgware overnight. In the morning we set off for St Albans. Again we set up camp and got down to some serious training. I fired a rifle for the first time and stuck bayonets into innumerable sandbags. It was a bit of fun; we were home defence and there was hardly any likelihood of there being any bloody Germans in England.

Posters everywhere asked for volunteers to 'fight for king and country'. Assembled one day we were asked whether we would like to volunteer for service abroad. Almost to man we said yes. Patriotism was at fever pitch. We were told that a fully-trained British soldier was worth five or six Germans. The regiment's padre gave us his blessing and said that we were going to fight for God as well as king and country. I wondered what the German troops were being told, after all Germany was a Christian nation, but I didn't ask. In the circumstances it would have sounded like high treason. We

Impressions of War

stayed at St Albans until January 1915. I managed to get a few days' leave at Christmas and when at home I had a long chat with Becky. We both knew it was only a matter of time before I'd be posted abroad and it might be a long time before we'd see each other again. We got engaged.

I travelled back to St Albans with Ted Smith. During our training Bernard Wetherall had opted to be transferred to the Royal Flying Corps. Our regiment was ordered to France. The war hadn't been concluded in the predicted fortnight, and the Allies faced the Germans on the Western Front. We embarked at Southampton and a few hours later I stepped ashore in France – the first time in my life I'd been out of England. Two weeks later we were in the trenches, having our baptism of fire. At that time no steel helmets were issued and we wore peaked caps. Most of us were pretty scared when we heard the shells and bullets. We didn't need to be told to 'keep our heads down'.

Eventually, when steel helmets were issued in 1916 there were not enough for everyone. As each battalion went into the front line it borrowed helmets from the battalion coming out. The War Office published a statement, reported in Parliament, that all British troops had been issued with them. This proved to be a piece of deliberate propaganda. Even when the lie had been exposed it took many months before there were sufficient helmets to go around.

In March 1915 we lay in reserve at the battle of Neuve Chapelle, just behind the front line. We were close enough to come under fire. The bullets didn't worry us much but the whine of a shell did. You just waited and hoped it wasn't going to land anywhere near you. Gurka troops were deployed. They suffered terribly, from not only heavy casualties but also the intense cold weather. They came out of the line, their normally brown faces grey with fatigue and cold.[1]

---

[1] In the Battle of Neuve Chapelle four British divisions of 40,000 men were committed along a 3 km front at 7.30 am on 10 March. Their advance was preceded by a 35-minute artillery bombardment of 342 guns across a 2,000

Called to the Colours

Group from the Royal West Surrey Regiment

Taken in France sometime in March-May 1915, Herbert Hodgson is kneeling, second from the right. The soldier kneeling on the extreme left is Alfred Rouse, who was hung for murder in 1931.[2]

Our first front-line engagement was at the battle of Festubert in May 1915. The cold weather had given way to spring rain and we were having our first experience of Flanders mud. I had thought that laying in reserve at Neuve Chapelle had been pretty scary but now

---

yard line, directed in part by reconnaissance aircraft from the Royal Flying Corps. More shells were discharged in that bombardment than in the whole of the Boer War. As well as Gurkas, soldiers from the British Indian Corps made up half the attacking force in battle. The assault was halted on 13 March after recapturing just over 2 km of lost ground. There were 4,200 Indian and 7,000 British casualties. The Germans lost a similar number.

[2] In the Battle of Festubert in May 1915, Rouse confronted a German soldier, lunged at him with his bayonet, but missed. On the last day of the battle a shell exploded nearby. He recuperated from severe head and thigh injuries in hospital, and was discharged from the army in 1916. (Source: http://en.wikipedia.org/wiki/Alfred_Rouse. Accessed 11 June 2010.)

Impressions of War

we were right in the front line. There was a continual bombardment from the German artillery and thousands of shells screamed overhead. I remember thinking that we had not been conditioned for this during training. Now I realise that this was the first time that a war had been fought in this way, two great armies facing each other for months, eventually years, across a few hundred yards of territory, hurtling destruction at each other.

It was all strangely exciting, despite the fear. We were patriots to a man, fighting for England with God on our side. It took some of us some time to appreciate that the Scots, Welsh and Irish regiments fighting alongside didn't quite see it that way. They weren't fighting for England but Great Britain. That was a bit of a puzzle to chaps like me, brought up in the streets of London. Surely England was Great Britain, I said to myself? Anyway, there we were in the front line and with the continual roar of the shells sounding like a never-ending London underground train. The division on our left was ordered over the top – up out of the trenches to charge across no-man's-land between us and the German lines. Most of them were cut down by machine guns which the Germans had concealed in no-man's-land during the night. Those that did get across came up against barbed wire and were picked off by German infantrymen. Three times during all this we were ordered to fix bayonets in readiness to go over the top ourselves but each time the order was cancelled. We weren't told why. Presumably it was considered fruitless to throw more troops over to almost certain death.[3]

We were ordered out of the front line and we marched back a few miles to a village. Most of the inhabitants had fled from the fighting and the army had commandeered buildings as billets for the troops. About fifty of us were allocated the village hall. The sun came out, it was very quiet and suddenly the war seemed far away. The village was on the La Bassée Canal and one afternoon several of us went for

---

[3] The Battle of Festubert of 15-25 May 1915 saw the first British army night attack of the war and resulted in the capture of the village. But the offensive achieved only 1 km of advance at a cost of 16,000 casualties.

a swim. I remember saying to Ted Smith that the water tasted a little better than the Surrey Canal.

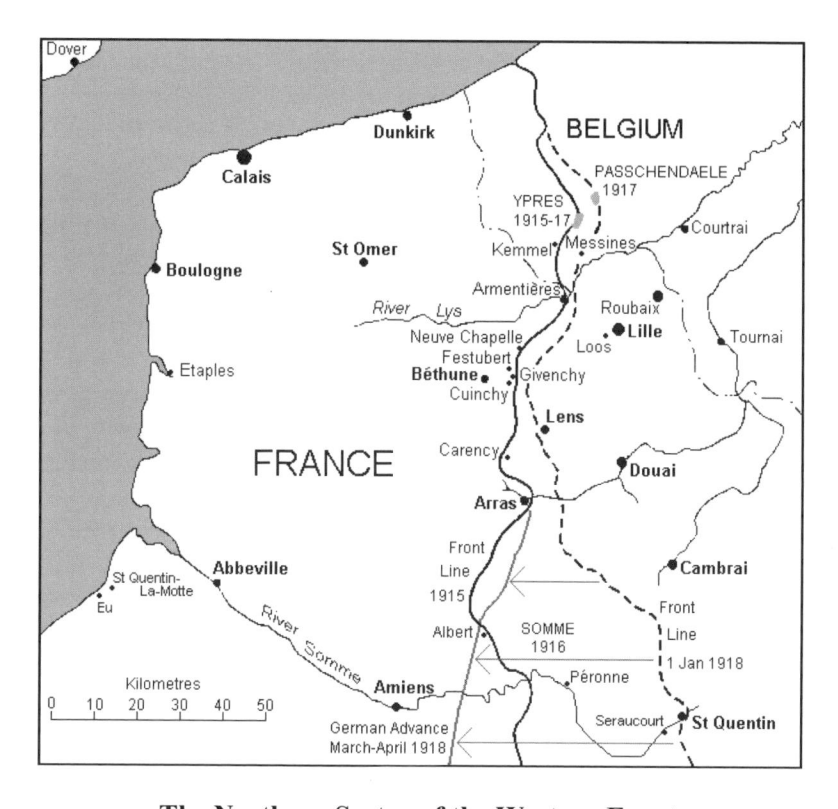

The Northern Sector of the Western Front

Our swim was interrupted by the command: 'Get back to your billets and dress in full battle order.' This could mean only one thing: we were going back into the line and probably over the top for the first time. With mixed feelings we fell in on the road and marched off. One of the men had a good voice and he started us singing for all we were worth. We were allowed to smoke as we marched. The singing and the smoking helped quell our apprehension. Finally came the order: 'No noise or smoking.' We were nearing the line.

Impressions of War

Group from the Royal West Surrey Regiment

Taken in France sometime in 1915-17, Herbert Hodgson is seated extreme left.

The scene was Givenchy, in the last few days of May 1915. We scrambled to our positions in the trenches and got the scaling ladders ready. Our artillery was hard at it, bombarding the German front line. At a given signal they lifted their sights and concentrated on the German rear, to stop reinforcements coming up. Then a whistle would blow in our section, and that would be the signal for us. That first time of waiting for the whistle was unforgettable. In some ways it was worse than actually going over the top. Tension, fear, excitement – we were gripped by them all. At last the whistle blew and we were over. I ran a few steps, tripped over our own barbed wire and went down. I thought at first that I'd been hit but I couldn't feel anything, so I got up and carried on. My comrades were falling all around me, some just keeling over without a sound, others screaming. Suddenly I found myself right up to the German lines. Luckily a number of others had managed it as well. The few

Called to the Colours

Germans remaining threw up their arms and surrendered. I looked at them. Like us, they were covered in mud and had no steel helmets.[4]

It had been surprisingly easy 'til now. The hard part was to come. After taking an enemy trench position, you had to hold it against the inevitable counter-attack. Our own artillery had made quite a mess of the trench and we had to set to with repairs. Meanwhile the German artillery had got the range and was showering us with shells. German snipers had taken up positions in trees watching for heads to go up. We were filling up sand bags and placing them in the breaches in the trench walls. I had just put one down when an enemy sniper must have noticed my movement. The next chap put his sand bag on top of mine and caught a bullet in the head. He was the lad with the fine voice who had led our singing just a short time before.

We held the trench for a night and day against four counter-attacks. Twenty-one-year-old Lance-Corporal Leonard Keyworth won the Victoria Cross in that battle.[5] He threw over a hundred German hand bombs back at them, helped by Captain Donald Figg, who was awarded the Distinguished Service Order for his bravery.[6]

---

[4] Alan H. Maude observed: 'the first advance was made by the 23rd and 24th London Battalions, who swept across the open ground just like a field-day attack at St Albans, and at once captured, with comparatively small losses, the German trenches opposite to them. But they then encountered a fierce and deadly enfilading fire from the German guns' (*The 47th (London) Division, 1914-1919*. London: Amalgamated Press, 1922, p. 19).

[5] Keyworth was awarded the VC by King George V at Buckingham Palace on 12 July 1915. His citation reads: 'For most conspicuous bravery at Givenchy on the night of 25-26 May 1915. After the successful assault on the German position by the 24th Battalion, London Regiment, efforts were made by that unit to follow up their success by a bomb attack, during the progress of which fifty-eight men out of a total of seventy-five became casualties. During this very fierce encounter L/Cpl Keyworth stood fully exposed for two hours on the top of the enemy's parapet, and threw about 150 bombs amongst the Germans, who were only a few yards away.'

[6] Figg's DSO citation reads: 'For conspicuous and continuous gallantry on the night of 25-26 May 1915, and following day, at Givenchy, when after

Impressions of War

Keyworth came from Lincoln and there is a memorial to him in Lincoln Cathedral. Keyworth died of wounds at Abbeville in October 1915, Figg at Clery on the Somme in March 1917.

In proportion to their numbers there were more officers killed than other ranks. They had to lead by example and they were always the first over the top leading the charge across no-man's-land. I was told once that the average expectation of life for an officer in the front line was only ten days. The hand bombs on both sides were made in the field. This was at the beginning of the war, before Mills bombs had been invented. Ours were made from jam tins filled with explosive and with a rag fuse stuffed in them. The German bombs took between six and ten seconds to explode and were often flung straight back at them.

During the afternoon of that day in the captured German trench a shell came over and blew the parapet in. One chap was killed instantly, two were seriously wounded and I was buried in debris with a shrapnel injury to my knee. I was quite conscious and could hear a voice saying: 'There's no-one else here.' I couldn't move and could hardly breathe but felt a cold current of air across one of my fingers. I wriggled it and another voice shouted 'There's someone here mate, quick, give me a hand.' I was dug out, put on a stretcher, carried back across no-man's-land to our own trenches and then taken by horse and limber to a field hospital. I was in hospital for about a month. The knee injury was not much more than a scratch, but I was also suffering from neurasthenia or 'shell shock'. I couldn't hear very well and seemed to be in a perpetual daze. The slightest

---

taking part in an assault on a trench, he led repeated rushes with bombs into a German work, and when most of the bombers were killed continued the attack single-handed. His extraordinary bravery and disregard of danger enabled the dangerous flank he commanded to hold its own against constant assaults by the German bombers and riflemen. On May 26th, when his line was enfiladed by rifle and very heavy shell fire, his determination held his men to their ground until relieved four hours later. For seventeen hours his conduct was a brilliant example to the hard-pressed men around him, and more than anyone in the battalion he contributed to the successful retention of the position won.'

Called to the Colours

noise startled me. I didn't like to make a fuss about it. Even at that early stage of the war there were already plenty of people ready to accuse one of malingering or even cowardice, and the penalties could be pretty severe.

The army was never slow to let the news travel along the line that another poor devil had been court-martialled, found guilty of desertion or cowardice and shot by a firing squad. It was a way to encourage the rest of us to 'do better'. At first I had no sympathy for such people but as the war dragged on my views changed. I saw men, decent likeable comrades, cowed and trembling at the thought of going into battle again and I could identify with how they felt. It didn't take much to turn such a man into a deserter. I was sent back to my battalion but from then on shell fire had a particular terror for me. When I got back I was told that before I had been blown up another shell had killed a courier in no-man's-land who was on his way with a rum ration for us.

Gradually we became accustomed to the nightmarish conditions of the front line, the mud and vermin, days on end soaked to the skin, and a monotonous diet of bread, corned beef, jam and gallons of tea. There was the continuous noise of machine guns, rifle fire and artillery shells. Going up the trenches at night, groping along on the duck boards in single file and hoping that the chap in front would not lose his footing on the front end of a board and tip the other end up in your face, mud and all. There would sometimes be a stifled curse when this happened, but often no sound at all, the chap on the receiving end being too tired of it all to be able to raise the energy.

When a shell whistled over and crashed nearby, I don't mind admitting I was scared. Rifle or machine gun fire did not frighten me, although they were more deadly. Other chaps felt the same. But if you had been hit by bullets in the past, then you were more scared by them than shells. Of course, the human body was never made to stand up to such things and one had to steel oneself to it all.

Narrow escapes were all in a day's work. When I first arrived; a corporal and three of us were talking together. A German sniper fired at us and the bullet hit the corporal's bayonet scabbard. Another time, in an attack, about six of us were ordered to jump over the top

Impressions of War

of a trench. Five caught a packet and I was the only one not hit. Incidentally, at a reunion of the Old Comrades Association after the war, I recounted this episode and one of the chaps told me he was one of the five wounded.

One time in the transport section, I was carrying my saddle and harness on my shoulders to the horse lines when a heavy 'Jack Johnson' shell burst a distance away and a large fragment whistled down in front of me and embedded itself in a brick wall.[7] Another step forward, and I would have caught it in the groin or stomach.

At night there would be a lull in the firing and those that were not on guard duty would settle down in whatever shelter they could find and try to sleep. Repairing the trenches at night was a nasty business. Carrying sheets of corrugated iron on our backs you could feel the bullets bouncing off. Along the back sides of the trenches were constructed crude dug-outs propped up with whatever pieces of timber we could find. The dug-outs weren't very big, always damp and would become crammed full at night but the proximity of so many bodies produced a bit of warmth. Even so it is not easy to rest comfortably on hard ground when you are cold and wet through, blankets and all, as seemed to be the norm. First thing in the morning as soon as it was light enough to get a fire going without it being too easy a target and the first mug of tea was brewing, the German guns would open up. There would be shouts of 'Thanks Jerry for the eggs with our bacon,' or 'For Christ's sake Jerry let's get breakfast over before we start work.' We lightened our troubles with such humour.

Every few days we would be relieved by another battalion and marched back to our billets, usually cattle barns and sheds. By the next morning we would be expected to have scraped all the mud and filth from our uniforms and smartened ourselves up ready for a parade and inspection. The worst problem as far as parades were concerned was the lice in our clothes. We all wore long woollen

---

[7] Jack Johnson (1878-1946) became the first black world heavyweight boxing champion in 1908. His name was used to describe German 15cm heavy artillery shells that produced a lot of black smoke. A 'Jack Johnson' was said to be 'big and black and knocked you to the ground.'

Called to the Colours

underwear which attracted the lice and sleeping on old straw in the billets seemed to compound the problem. Candles were on issue to us and we'd try getting rid of the lice by running a lighted candle up the seams and creases of our clothes. You could hear the eggs popping but you never got rid of them all. It was almost impossible to stand still on parade when you felt something crawling up the middle of your back or the more delicate parts of your body. People at home used to send boxes of Keating's Powder and other insect killers but we swore the blighters thrived on the stuff and got fatter.

We always carried what were called our 'iron rations', a tin of corned beef (known as bully beef), a small portion of tea, sugar and some biscuits, all in a little white bag. Iron rations were only to be eaten in an emergency. When in billets behind the line we used to hang the bags up on the beams of the barn, hoping that the rats couldn't get at them. If someone had said to me before I went to France that there would come a time when I would be so tired that I'd sleep with rats running all over me, then I'd have laughed in their face. One night we had all settled down when suddenly there was a terrific yell from the chap alongside me. Someone lit a candle and we found him with blood all over his face and with a big lump swelling on his forehead. A rat had managed to get to his iron ration bag and had gnawed through it. When the hole was large enough however the rations had dropped through and the one pound tin of bully beef had hit him fair and square. The poor devil didn't get much sympathy, everyone swearing at him for waking us up.

When out of the line we would parade for baths. Rudimentary cold showers were provided. Anyone who funked having a shower would suffer the ignominy and agony of being forcibly thrust under the cold water and 'washed' with a scrubbing brush. It may sound brutal but it was only fair on everyone else, one dirty person could spread sickness and disease. I was standing under a shower once, together with a number of others, when I noticed a chap staring intently at me. I stared back at him when he suddenly said: 'Your name is Hodgson, isn't it?' After a few seconds I recognised him. It was our old Scoutmaster, Mr Woodgate. I hadn't seen him since he disappeared on our ill-fated hike to Sevenoaks. Little did I dream

Impressions of War

then that the next time we were to meet would be in our birthday suits on foreign soil.

Woodgate was a stretcher bearer. A couple of weeks later he was severely wounded in the spine at Cuinchy brickfields. It was night and he was carrying a wounded officer. It was also at Cuinchy in February 1915 that Michael O'Leary of the Irish Guards regiment won the Victoria Cross. He single-handedly charged and destroyed two German barricades defended by machine-gun positions.

Hearing that Mr Woodgate had been wounded I asked my officer for permission to see him before he was carted off on a stretcher. My request was refused. I was a little relieved. I didn't fancy being on that stretch of road at that time, but I felt I was doing the right thing. The road ran from Béthune to La Bassée and was lined with trees. Even on the darkest night the line of trees made an easy target for German machine guns or snipers. All they had to do was aim low down and the bullets would either miss them or ricochet off.

In that sector the water table was too high for trenches to be dug, so branches, twigs and sandbags were used to build the sides. This made an easy target for the Germans. In the winter, with snow and ice about, it was sheer hell. We were issued with whale oil to rub on our feet but many a poor devil was taken out with frost-bitten hands and feet and trench fever. During the first part of the war we were always short of guns, ammunition and men. The troops would be spread out along the line trying to deceive the Germans. Every time we attacked we were told our objective was to advance to a point some miles behind the German lines. It never worked. We would go forward a couple of miles, hold the position for a day or so, suffer frightening casualties and then there would be a counter-attack and we'd be driven back to where we had started.

This was to be the pattern, month after month, year after year. In front of our line we dug trenches called saps, reaching out into no-man's-land. They were used for reconnaissance and guard duty. Tin cans would be scattered about the ground at the end of the sap and a rifle was mounted on a tripod pointing down it. When on guard duty we were ordered to fire the rifle down the sap if any noise was heard. One night three of us were detailed out of the front line trench for

Called to the Colours

duty there. That night the heavens opened. There was no cover and soon we were soaked to the skin. Our two hours of duty stretched to three and there was no sign of a relieving party. Finally the corporal sent the other chap back to find out why. He found the front line deserted! Our battalion had been due to be relieved. There were lines of communication trenches running behind the front line. A battalion being relieved filed along one set while the relieving party came up another. Each battalion was guided by a scout and the scouts were supposed to liaise with one another to ensure the front line was never empty. In this instance the scouts had lost touch with each other in the rain and darkness and the front line was left unmanned. If the Germans had launched an offensive at that moment they would have run all over us in the sap and taken a good deal of ground as well.

No-man's-land, between us and the Germans, was not an empty stretch of barren landscape as the name might imply. We were fighting on farmland meadows that, a few months before, had been a scene of rustic tranquillity. Many of the buildings had disappeared, blasted to smithereens by the constant exchange of shellfire. I remember one place near La Bassée where the only thing left standing was the farmyard pump. We called the area 'Dead Cow Farm' because the rotting carcase of a cow lay nearby, another victim of the war.[8] The pump, still in working order, was much nearer to our lines than the Germans' and we used to get our water supplies from it. But being detailed to fetch water was not a task to

---

[8] More precisely, Dead Cow Farm was about 1 km east of Festubert. Robert Graves (1895-1985), who served in the area in 1915, wrote a poem entitled 'Dead Cow Farm', with the lines:
    Here now is chaos once again,
    Primeval mud, cold stones and rain
    Here flesh decays and blood drips red,
    And the Cow's dead, the old Cow's dead.
His autobiographical *Goodbye to All That* (1929) covers his experiences in the First World War, including incidents at Festubert, Cuinchy, Loos and High Wood. In 1927 Graves also published a biography of T. E. Lawrence.

Impressions of War

be relished. The German snipers had the pump pin-pointed. The pump handle creaked and even in the dark it was pretty risky being out there. Many of our chaps caught a packet. One night I had a near miss when a bullet hit the pump as I was working its handle.

My old friend Ted Smith had an interest in horses and had been granted a transfer into the battalion transport section. My other old chum, Bernard Wetherall, was still in England stationed on the Essex coast. Both Ted and I corresponded with him. Years later Bernard showed me two letters that I wrote to him:

Pte H J Hodgson
No 1 Platoon A Co
1/24th Lon Regt
2nd Lon Div TF
BEF, GPO London

Dear Bern,

Just a few lines in answer to your letter. Glad to hear you are going on alright and hope you get into the munition works, it must be disappointing for you Bern because you are not able to come out, but still cheer up it is not your fault and besides you're better off where you are at Frinton-on-Sea. We have had a draft from the 2nd Batt. out. I was talking to one of the chaps this morning the name of Cole; he was billeted with you at Bishops Stortford. He lives over Walthamstow and wishes to be remembered to you.

We are in the trenches again, been in for 10 days now right off. We are being relieved though now very shortly by another Div and I expect we shall go back and have a rest, and it is rumoured about leave, but still you know what rumours are.

Dear Bern I couldn't help laughing about what you said about Ted's letter he sent you, his brain ought to be alright because he has never been in the trenches yet, he is one of our Captains grooms, a cushy time looking after one horse.

Dear Bern I got nearly to seeing your cousin Bill Barclamb the other week. When I was in the hospital there was a RGA in there as well, McCarthy by name he said your cousin was his chum, and he told me that their battery had been attached to our Div for

Called to the Colours

some time. He said he would ask Bill to look out for our Batt. I wonder whether he knew he was attached to the lot I was in.
Thanks for the photos, they were very welcome.
Well Bern I think I will now close. As I am writing this our guns and old Fritz's guns are having a go at each other, their usual morning hate, only the worst of it is some of the souvenirs drop in our trenches. You can bet it keeps us busy dodging them.
With kindest regards to your mother and Dad etc.
I remain
Your old chum
Bert

I often saw Ted Smith when resting behind the line and through him I picked up a little knowledge of horses. I decided I would apply for a transfer into the transport section and managed to convince the transport officer that I was quite expert although I had never ridden a horse in my life. It was at this time that I wrote another letter to Bernard Wetherall. It was 1916 and patriotism was still at fever pitch at home with many writers, a contributor to the *John Bull* magazine amongst them, forecasting that Germany would capitulate soon. There was optimism too among the British troops that the German army could not possible survive another winter, optimism born more of hope than expectation:

Pte H J Hodgson
Transport Section
1/24th Lon Regt
BEF France

Dear Bern,
Just a few lines to thank you for the cigs and John Bull. It is very well thought out about what he says, but still I think that is a ruse for recruiting. Of course there is no doubt that Germany must be getting under while we are getting in our prime, but if you were out here to see how they counter-attack to get back their lost trenches they are not whacked yet. And to drive them back across the Rhine it will take a hell of a lot of guns and men.

Impressions of War

But us chaps reckon this winter will do the Germans, let's hope it will because we all of us are just about fed up, but still we don't mind sticking it rather than see old England go under.

I was glad you went to see my people and was pleased to hear my mum and dad are better in health.

Well Bern our Batt. is coming out of the trenches again and going back for a good rest and it is supposed to be 'official' about leave again. Ted and myself couldn't help smiling when you said you went home on leave. I don't blame you trying to get a chance of going abroad if you can.

About Marie's parcel Bern. Well she sent a packet of cigs some time ago and in the letter she sent she said she was going to send a cake the next week. I sent her a letter thanking her for the cigs but as I never received the cake I didn't know what to do so it must have got lost or broken on the way out here.

I was glad Beck went over and enjoyed herself. I reckon they must be sick of being on their own.

That chap Pearce you were talking about, well we had two chaps in our platoon, one was wounded in the Givenchy charge, Percy Pearce, and the other, Tom Pearce, was killed. I think the one you know was Percy Pearce, he had a brother who was a bit of a devil. They were both wounded and as far as I know they are in Angleterre.

Dear Bern we did go to some weddings to remember, Vesta's one where we had such a ripping dinner and tea.

Ted sends his best respects to you Bern, he is not a groom now, his job is riding and driving a limber. I am trying for it as well. I am writing this just inside our bivouac with the wind and rain playing hell all round. Old Ted is cleaning his bayonet up and we have got a nice little coke fire so we are not so bad off.

Well Bern I think I will close now with best respects to your mother and dad.

I remain
Your sincere chum
Bert

Called to the Colours

The army relied heavily on horses. Motorised transport was still in its infancy as a means of military communication in war and all the heavy fetching and carrying was done by limbers, two separate wagons joined together. The wagons were easily detachable and much better over rough ground and shell holes than a single long wagon. Each limber was pulled by a team of two horses, the driver of the limber riding the nearside horse and controlling both on short reins. The harness and traces were quick release with detachable links half way along the horses' flanks. In danger or retreat, or if a limber got stuck in the mud, the driver could release his team, the spare man could mount the other horse and all could get away. One hazard was the centre pole, which was constantly flying up on the rough terrain and so each driver wore a leg iron strapped to his right leg to protect him.

Much as men suffer in war it can be as nothing compared with horses. Men have an understanding; horses have none. Men can recover from wounds but in many cases horses have to be shot. The sights and sounds of the suffering of horses on the Western Front will never leave my mind. Like all other drivers, I became devoted to my charges. They always came first, a view endorsed somewhat cynically by the army: 'Your horses always come first. You can get a good soldier for a shilling a day but a good horse costs twenty to thirty pounds!' Every limber driver gave names to his horses. One of mine had a white blaze on his face and I called him Snowy. The other could never stand still but would raise each foot in turn in an almost rhythmic movement. I called him Tango. The winters were especially hard for the horses. We could usually find a dugout or an old barn, but the horses were simply tethered outside. After a cold and wet night we'd find that they had kicked the mud away from their hind legs and their hind quarters were a foot or two down in the ground while their fronts were up in the air. Sometimes they would be so frozen that we'd have to walk them about gently to get some circulation going. We'd then mount them bareback and guide them to a nearby stream for a drink. Often the water would be frozen and the ice had to be broken. This of course was before we got a fire going for ourselves and put a lump of ice in the pot for our first cup

Impressions of War

of tea. We had to be careful about their food. There was a scare once that some imported corn and oats had been tampered with by German agents who had mixed tin tacks into the sacks. We were ordered to inspect the contents of each sack and look at each grain before feeding the horses.

Mules were introduced later. They were obstinate creatures and more uncomfortable to ride. A piece of paper blowing about would make them shy and gallop away but when the shells and bullets were flying about and you wanted them to run they stood rooted to the spot. With horses we used snaffle bits, with mules it was bar bits but it made no difference, they only moved when it suited them. They were tougher than horses and didn't suffer from horse ailments such as greasy heels, saddle galls and breast galls.

Life in the transport section was a little easier than being an infantryman. We didn't have to rough it in the trenches but we had our share of danger. Our job was to get supplies of food and ammunition to the front line and most of our work was done at night. During the Battle of Loos we had to go between the German and our own lines and to deaden the noise we tied old motor tyres around our steel-rimmed wheels. Sergeant Soper, an old Boer War veteran, was in charge. He gave the orders quietly and each limber in turn would make a dash for it, full speed across no-man's-land. When it came to my turn I dug in my spurs and took off. All went well and I had nearly reached our lines when the tyres fell off. The noise on the road was horrific. A German machine gun opened up and hit the limber but miraculously the horses and I got through unscathed.

In the Battle of Loos, which lasted for three days in September 1915, the British army suffered as many casualties as it did during the whole of the Boer War, which lasted for three years.[9] Such a scale of carnage! Rumours were rife in those early battles. The

---

[9] Following a four-day artillery bombardment in which 250,000 shells were fired, the Loos offensive began on 25 September and was called off in failure on 28 September. During the battle the British suffered 50,000 casualties. German casualties were estimated at approximately half the British total. During this battle Rudyard Kipling's son Jack was killed.

Called to the Colours

Germans had retreated twenty miles, the French had broken through on the right etc.. But in reality a few yards of ground had been won, which eventually would be lost again. Infantrymen could duck into a dug-out when the shelling was particularly heavy but we had to stand by our charges, hoping that a shell wouldn't land on top of us or on the road nearby. The roads were cobbled and pieces of stone would fly around with the shrapnel after a shell had landed. In soft mud the shells didn't explode, they were percussion shells, but you'd hear the thud nearby and wait for the explosion. We'd stroke our horses and steady them but I can't deny having the wind up.

Hellfire Corner, Menin Road, near Ypres

The Menin Road in the Ypres Salient was sheer hell. The British army held the Salient for four years. The Germans were in command of the hills around and we were in the open, on level ground. Our casualties were colossal. We were strafed wherever we were and we named some of the worst stretches of road 'Shrapnel Corner' and 'Hellfire Corner'. A lighter moment came when one of our drivers 'found' a 36-gallon barrel of French beer. It was nothing like English ale but very welcome nonetheless. Every day we lined up for our

Impressions of War

'cuppa' and it lasted quite a while. When the last drop was served one of our lads, completely sozzled, wrapped his arms around the barrel and sung his favourite song: 'Sweet Robert Emmett'.

One night I'd driven the rations up to the lads in the trenches and was on my way back to the horse lines when I noticed something beside the road. It was soaked through with rain. As I hoisted it up onto my cart it burst open. My two horses and I were enveloped in white flour, but I saved some of it. I remounted and gave the horses their rein. As I approached our lines the chap on picket duty came along. He told me I'd given him the fright of his life. All he could see in the darkness was a white apparition, a phantom pair of horses with a driver astride one of them. He thought it was a ghost train. But I earned the gratitude of the rest of the troops. The cook was able to make something in the way of a 'spotted dick'. We called spotted dick 'windmill pudding' – if it went round far enough you got a bit!

I had taken an old banjo to France (it went right through the war with me) and a couple of chaps had mouth organs, so we often had impromptu concerts and got a sing-song going.

In the early part of 1916, after twelve months in France, the rumour of leave I'd mentioned in my letter to Bernard Wetherall became a reality and I was granted seven days in 'dear old Blighty'. We who were going on leave were greatly excited and were driven on limbers to our regimental base some miles away. When we got there a sergeant addressed us: 'You're all bloody filthy and flea-ridden. Get in that shed over there and get de-loused. We can't have you goin' 'ome like that.' It was a bit deflating but we filed into the shed and were each squirted all over with some powder. We then had to wait around for some time before the substance worked and we could have a shower and clean up. We caught a boat at Calais and disembarked at Southampton. From Waterloo I got a tram. When I offered the fare the conductor waved it away: '''ave this one on me.'

The seven days soon went by. Every evening at six o'clock I met Becky when she finished work at the pickle factory and walked her home. We talked about getting married but decided that we should wait until the war was over. 'It can't last more than another six months' I told her, not very convincingly. One night during that week we went to the Oxford Music Hall and saw a play by Bruce Bairnsfather. He had created the cartoon character of 'Old Bill', a soldier serving on the Western Front, who was always looking for a 'better 'ole' in which to rest. Seeing that play was like a busman's holiday for me! The high spot of the week was seeing George Robey and Violet Lorraine at the London Hippodrome. They were appearing in a revue – I think it was called 'Zig Zag' – and they sang 'If You Were the Only Girl in the World' together. That was a show stopper! I said goodbye to Becky and my parents at eight o'clock one morning and twelve hours later I was back on the Western Front.

British Mark I Tank at the Somme, September 1916

Conscription was introduced during the first part of 1916 and suddenly the Front seemed to be flooded with men. British industry had been geared up to serve the war effort and there was an abundance of guns and ammunition. We soon found out why. The Battle of the Somme started in July 1916. This was it – we told ourselves – the battle that would end the war. The first offensive had some success. The Germans were pushed back to the gates of Péronne. After that, progress was much slower.

Trenches at the Somme, 1916

In September our division, the 47th London Infantry, took part in a new offensive. Armoured tanks, one of the best kept secrets of the war, were used for the first time. They gave the Germans quite a surprise, smashing right over their machine-gun posts.[10] Great

---

[10] On 15 September 1916 Hodgson's division captured the notorious death trap of High Wood, 10 km east of Albert. 4,500 men in the division were killed. Its commander, Major-General Barter, was dismissed by Lieutenant-General Pulteney for 'wanton waste of men'. But it seems that Barter was a scapegoat for the errors of those above him. A tank used on that day remained rusting in High Wood until the 1960s. (See Terry Norman, *The Hell They Called High Wood,* Barnsley: Pen and Sword, 2009.)

advances were made but, as always, with frightful casualties, the territory gained was as nothing compared with the human misery. And then the rains came. The area became a quagmire. The whole British army in that sector of the fighting got stuck in the mud.[11]

Our horses, floundering in the morass, would struggle until they were up to their withers and the drivers' boots and stirrups in it as well. One night on the road near Carency we'd driven our limbers up to the front line with rations and ammunition and were on our way back to the transport lines. There were several convoys on the road including artillery ammunition columns. Suddenly the German artillery started up and shells were raining down all around. A driver at the front of our line let his team have it and it acted as a signal for the whole of the convoys. Away we all went at full gallop, shells bursting, sparks flying, complete bedlam!

After the Somme we settled in for another winter. It turned out to be the worst we were to suffer throughout the war. We had snow and ice right through until March 1917. One morning I had just refilled a water limber with 110 gallons and was about to mount my nearside horse when my foot slipped on the ice. The two horses bolted and pulled the limber right over my buttocks. It was excruciating, I can tell you. I wasn't very pleased either at being told by the army doctor who first examined me: 'It's possible you may never father a child.' Anyway that packet got me back to Blighty again, this time to a military hospital in York. I had a pretty rough time of it but it was like heaven to be sleeping in a bed between sheets. After that I was sent for a month's convalescence at Cloughton, six miles from Scarborough. Lord Airdale's estate had been turned over to the army and fourteen of us, all from different regiments, lived in the big house. A matron and two nurses, all volunteers, looked after us.

But there were rules to obey and matron was pretty strict. With hindsight she had a job to do and we shouldn't have played her up so much. But she made us feel like little boys. Being freed from the rigours of the front line, we were intent on enjoying ourselves. We

---

[11] The Battle of the Somme, from July to November 1916, was one of the bloodiest conflicts in history, with an estimated 1.5 million casualties.

Impressions of War

liked to visit a pub in the village, but we had to be in by ten o'clock. We arranged that if one of our number stayed out later we'd let him in through a window. But one night a chap was half way through the window when the matron came in and saw him. He was so startled he fell through, taking the glass and glazing bars with him. We had the cost of repairs docked from our pay. During a sing-song by the piano in the library one night, one chap, a brilliant impersonator, had us in fits of laughter giving us his impression of matron. He joined the pianist in a very funny piano duet. They were making a frightful din, when someone threw a book at them. That was the signal for the rest of us: books, cushions, wicker chairs all rained down on them until they were covered but they played on, still playing when matron walked in. The audience fell silent as she gave everybody a verbal blast. We were banned from the library for a while.

Came the time when six of us were declared fit to return to our units. We said our goodbyes and climbed aboard an army truck. We had just arrived at the railway station when one chap produced the keys of the house. He had pinched them before departing and promptly dropped them down a nearby drain: 'Now she won't be able to lock up at nights and the chaps can stay out as long as they bleedin' want.' I've often wondered what matron said in response.

I reported to my battalion headquarters at Kennington and was sent to Winchester for retraining. I was still quite lame and went on light duties until pronounced fully fit. After a course of signalling I passed out as a first-class signaller. Meanwhile I had been home a number of times and Becky and I discussed marriage again. As I saw it, I would probably not be sent back to France. I never doubted the fact that we would win the war so why wait until it was all over to get married? She agreed and we were married on 15 September 1917 at St Mary Magdalene Church, Southwark.

For me the months rolled by rather pleasantly in 'dear old Blighty'. My regimental duties down at Winchester were hardly exacting and I could get home fairly frequently. The Western Front was a million miles away, although there was still no sign of the end. One day in March 1918, several of us were told the news we'd been dreading: we were being sent back to France.

Called to the Colours

Herbert and Rebecca Hodgson on their Wedding Day, 1917

Instead of returning to my old regiment I was drafted into the 9th Battalion of the Royal Irish Fusiliers. I had to get used to life in the trenches again. In the spring of 1918 the Germans were throwing everything at us. It was their last attempt to drive us right back to the Channel Ports.[12] We were constantly on the move, retreating one

---

[12] Hodgson alludes here to the German offensives around the Somme and Lys valleys in March and April 1918. Because of a German treaty with the new Communist Government in Russia, hostilities had ended in the east, thus freeing up German troops for the Western Front. Hodgson fought in both the Somme and Lys theatres of war in 1918. Tragically the German offensives of that year swept back over the ground at the Somme and Passchendaele that had been gained previously at such human cost.

Impressions of War

minute and going forward the next.[13] In one battle I was sent into a peasant house. It must have just been evacuated by the family; the stove was alight with a saucepan of hot coffee standing on it. I lifted it up and was about to take a swig when I felt a prod in my back. I was so startled I dropped the saucepan. There was silence. I still had my rifle in my right hand but no-one made a grab for it yet I fully expected that a couple of Germans had surprised me. There was another prod and I slowly turned around. The prodding was from a goat that must have followed me in from the farmyard outside.

For the second time I went over the top.[14] As with my first experience I fell after the first few yards, this time stumbling in a shell hole. I spread my arms and my hand grasped something in the mud. It was a book. I shoved it in my pocket, got up and carried on. I don't remember much else except hearing a loud bang. A shell had landed nearby and the blast had knocked me out. I was picked up by a stretcher party and carried back to the line. When I came to I remembered the book. It was a Bible. How long it had lain there I don't know but it was encrusted with mud. There was no name inside it but the army service number 34816 had been written across the top edges of the pages. I was sent back to a field hospital and there I told an officer about my find and asked what I should do with it. He told

---

[13] On the morning of 21 March 1918 the 9th Royal Irish Fusiliers were near Seraucourt-le-Grand near St Quentin on the Somme. An intensive artillery barrage preceded a massive enemy attack that forced them to retreat west 40 km over six days. Overall that was 'the bloodiest day of the First World War' with over 78,000 casualties on both sides. On 26 March the Germans captured the town of Albert. On 27 March the 9th Battalion marched west for recreation and training, mostly at Eu and St Quentin-la-Motte near Abbeville. On 10 April they returned to the front at Kemmel, near Ypres. (Sources: http://www.northirishhorse.net/ww1/rif.html#_ftnref45, accessed 8 June 2010; Ian Passingham, *The German Offensives of 1918*, Barnsley: Pen and Sword, 2008, pp. 47, 64.)

[14] Hodgson does not mention the time or location of this attack. From detailed available evidence (see footnote 15) it was likely to be between Wulverghem and Messines in Belgium, on 12 April 1918.

Called to the Colours

me that in the chaos going on it was pointless trying to find its rightful owner. 'I'd keep it if I were you,' he said, 'it might bring you luck.' It occurred to me that having come through unscathed after being blown up by a shell it might already have done just that.[15]

---

[15] That Bible was kept in the possession of Herbert Hodgson's family. Amazingly, 92 years later, its original owner was traced! Army service number 34816 was Private Richard Llewellyn Cook, of the Otago Regiment of the New Zealand Expeditionary Force, son of Reuben and Mary Jane Cook, of Colac Bay, Southland, New Zealand. Aged 26, he was shot in an attack on Gravenstafel Ridge near Passchendaele on 4 October 1917. He wrote to his parents on 7 October, telling them that he was in No. 7 Canadian General Hospital and wounded in his left hip and right shoulder. On the following day he bled to death on a stretcher. He is buried in Étaples Military Cemetery in France. (Sources: surviving relatives in New Zealand; http://freepages.genealogy.rootsweb.ancestry.com/~sooty/nzefrohco-cu.html and www.cwgc.org – web pages accessed 8 June 2010.)

During the War there were numerous British hospitals and reinforcement camps at Étaples. The New Zealand Expeditionary Force fought at Messines in June, at Polygon Wood near Ypres in September, and near Passchendaele in October 1917. Hodgson's battalion fought at the first of these only. It seems that Richard Cook lost his Bible near Messines.

The capture of the Messines Ridge was one of the most successful Allied operations of the War. It followed a huge explosion on 7 June 1917 – heard as far away as London and unrivalled until the atomic bombs of 1945 – caused by the detonation of mines in tunnels deep beneath the surface. The blast killed about 10,000 German soldiers and destroyed most of the fortifications on the ridge, as well as the town of Messines itself. This remains the deadliest man-made non-nuclear explosion in history.

But in their Lys Offensive the Germans recaptured Messines on 10 April 1918. Herbert Hodgson's Battalion moved on 11 April from Kemmel to 'Stinking Farm', 2 km south-west of Messines. On that critical day several German units broke through the lines and General Douglas Haig issued his famous order: 'With our backs to the wall and believing in the justice of our cause, each us must fight on to the end.' The entry for 12 April in the War Diary of the 9th Royal Irish Fusiliers notes their retreat: '2am Moved to near Wulverghem. Headquarters at N Midland Farm. Enemy attacked, pressing back our line. Counter attack completely restored position. Casualties heavy.' (Source: http://www.northirishhorse.net/ww1/rif.html#_ftnref45,

Impressions of War

I was kept in the hospital for some time, suffering from the delayed action of shell shock. Again I was in a daze most of the time and couldn't seem to concentrate for very long. The doctors kept examining me until one day one said that he thought my fighting days were over. 'From now on you're Category B3,' he told me. I was sent back right down the line and put on light duties again.[16]

Armistice came in November 1918 but it was February 1919 before I was sent to Dieppe to await a ship for Blighty. For a week we were encamped in snow on top of the cliffs, outwardly cold but inwardly exhilarated. We were going home for good, the 'war to end all wars' was over. But there was one more hitch. The boat taking us to Southampton had to lay in the Solent for four hours, unable to disembark because of a strike in the docks. Eventually we landed, entrained for Winchester and handed in our kit. We were out of the army at last! It was midnight and we asked the sergeant major if there were any trains to London: 'No lads, you'd better shake down here in the camp 'til morning.' 'No thanks,' we replied 'we've got our tickets at last and we've finished with army camps.' We walked out and slept on the station platform until the first train came in.

With millions of others, I had started fresh and keen as a volunteer, swinging down the lanes of Britain, singing all the choruses of the day, young and fit and ready for anything. But many a lad I knew did never return, and some of those that did were worn to a standstill.

---

accessed 8 June 2010.) As Ian Passingham (op. cit., p. 93) writes, the German 'leading battalions were rapidly stopped near Wulverghem by stiff British resistance and then counter-attacks.' Wulverghem is 3 km west of Messines. On 14 April the 9th Royal Irish Fusiliers moved back to Kemmel. Richard Cook's Otago Regiment had dug in around North Midland Farm from March to June 1917 (A. E. Byrne, *Official History of the Otago Regiment, N.Z.E.F. in the Great War 1914-1918*, Dunedin: Wilkie, 1921, pp. 159-61). He may have lost his Bible during heavy shelling at that time.

[16] May 1918 saw a large influx of US troops that helped to turn the tables against the Germans on the Western Front (Passingham, op. cit., p. 101).

3. Pillars of Wisdom

I was twenty-one when the war started, full of the innocence and expectation of youth. I had grown up with social degradation all around me but I had been one of the lucky ones. I'd never known what it was like to be really hungry or to live in a family atmosphere of despair and violence. At the end of the war I was twenty five and still one of the lucky ones: I had come through almost unscathed. Over 800,000 British servicemen had been killed and more than a million others were permanently disabled. But I had changed. My innocence had gone. I had become conscious of a social order which seemed so unfair to the majority of the population, a social order that I blamed for the carnage of the last four years.

In the years immediately prior to the war there had been great trials of strength between organised labour and the bosses. It had been a time of increasing prices but no corresponding rise in wages. The war had stopped the confrontation, but now the tide of resentment had returned. Before the war I hadn't taken much interest in what had been going on. Other things in my life had been far more absorbing. But now at twenty five I saw things differently. There was widespread unrest in industry. In the immediate aftermath of war there was a shortage of manpower. This, coupled with the increased cost of living, gave the green light for industrial struggle. Strikes once again proliferated, the main demands being for increased wages and reduced working hours. The 44 hour week became the demand throughout industry.

I went back to my old firm near Ludgate Circus. It was very strange working in a factory again. I attended evening classes to bring myself up to date. Things were changing. Machinery was becoming fully-automated and the old hand-feeding of the presses was disappearing. There was growing union representation in the printing industry and in due course I joined. But the union was not recognised by the firm and the wages were below the recommended

Impressions of War

union rate of the day. The day I joined the union I told our shop foreman that I now expected the union rate. He took me to see the manager. 'What's all this?' I was asked. 'I've joined the printer's union,' I replied. 'I don't care if you've joined the mother's union' snorted the manager 'You're not getting any extra here.' He gave me the choice of accepting or leaving. I left.

As I walked out I almost went back to say I'd changed my mind. On my way home on my bike I pondered on what I'd done. I was a married man with a child and I was very conscious of my new responsibilities. The army doctor's gloomy foreboding was proved wrong and my son Bert had been born in November 1919. I told my wife the whole story and of the misgivings I was feeling. She listened quietly and asked 'Why did you join the union?' I replied: 'To try to improve the wages and conditions of the working man.' Her answer was: 'Well, haven't you just taken a step towards that? You either believe in your principles or you don't.' That settled it. It was the most marvellous and supportive answer possible, from a mild-mannered and unmilitant person. I was now, more than ever, a convinced and dedicated trade unionist.

But it did not do me much good in finding another job. Jobs began to get scarce. Wages and prices actually went down. I became a jobbing printer, which meant reporting to the union headquarters at Blackfriars and being sent out to work for a specific time, usually a week or two, in a firm where they had some rush work on.

Our daughter Lilian was born in October 1921. We lived at 51 Azenby Road, Peckham in the upper part of the house occupied by my parents. I earned about three pounds ten shillings a week when I could get a full week's work. The rent of the house was ten shillings a week.[1] We managed fairly comfortably although there wasn't much left over after the bills were paid.

It was the time of the Means Test – the subjecting of applicants for state assistance to a minute examination of their domestic circumstances and finances. Becky's mother applied once and the woman who carried out the inspection said to her, after rummaging

---

[1] In 2010 prices the wages would be about £142 and the rent about £20.

Pillars of Wisdom

through every drawer, cupboard and receptacle in the house: 'Pawn your spare sheets. You've got one set on the beds.'

We went on occasional trips when we could afford it. Days out in London were interspersed with rail trips to the seaside, to Brighton in particular. In 1919 my union won the right to a weeks' annual paid holiday, a very rare concession. My father was astounded. He never thought he would live to see that. It was pleasant enough to have the time off and be paid for it, but there was not enough money for us to go very far. Holidays away from home had not yet become a way of life. Life for most was still a drudge, working 50 to 60 hours a week all year round, living in poor to squalid conditions and eating a monotonous diet, the general gloom being interspersed by Sundays and the few Bank Holidays.

After the Great War, union militancy fomented a change in attitudes. Our union agreed a 48 hour working week with the Employers Federation. Gradually over the next few years other unions won similar concessions. For the first time the state took responsibility for providing decent living accommodation. Lloyd George's famous call at the end of the War for 'homes fit for heroes' was activated by making local government authorities responsible for building houses. In fact the number of houses built in the first few years fell far short of the target. But the seed had been sown, and few argued against the principle of the state having such a responsibility.

Both Bernard Wetherall and Ted Smith had survived the war, married and settled down. Ted moved away from our area and we lost touch, but Bernard and Marie lived nearby. Bernard became a bus driver. With his shift work it was difficult for us to meet. But we decided that our musical activity should continue. So we formed another musical group. Popular music became influenced by the jazz craze in America and the invention of the phonograph record. We bought a record player and listened to this new music. It was not to our liking but we were impressed with the syncopated rhythm and the instrumentation. In addition to my banjo and Bernard's piano we recruited a saxophone and drums. We four were in great demand at local weddings. The older guests would press us to play the old tunes and the younger guests would ask us to 'hot it up'.

W. H. Smith Printing Department in 1922

Herbert Hodgson is in the second row from the front, second from the left

My jobbing printing work continued into 1923. Twice I worked at W. H. Smith's in Southwark. After the second time, Mr C. H. St. John Hornby, a partner and director of W. H. Smith, wrote to the union commending my work.[2] It was pleasing to hear but it meant little at the time. Not long after that it came to mean a great deal. I was up at Blackfriars one day and was told by the union secretary of a request for a printer at an address in Paddington. I was also told that because of the job description and the commendation of Mr Hornby, I was the only chap they could send. I asked what the job was and how long it was likely to be. The answer was not very

---

[2] C. H. St. John Hornby (1867-1946) was the founder of the Ashendene Press. He became a partner of W. H. Smith in 1893. In 1917 he was appointed by John Hodge, Minister of Labour, to the chairmanship of a labour-management conciliation board in the County of London. Hornby was offered a safe parliamentary seat but turned it down. A prominent participant in many philanthropic organizations, Hornby served for many years as the deputy vice chairman of the Society for the Prevention of Cruelty to Children. (Source: *Dictionary of Literary Biography*.)

encouraging. A chap had taken on the job of printing a private book on his own and wanted someone to give him advice on how to set it up and get started. Very undecided, I walked out of union headquarters. This doesn't sound like much of a job I thought, probably three weeks work and then out. I cycled up to Westminster Bridge and stood on the south side, looking across at Big Ben. Finally I decided to give it a go. After all, it was work of some sort.

The address to which I cycled was in Westbourne Terrace North at the Harrow Road end. It was a dingy-looking shop and there were other equally dingy-looking shops on either side of the street. I walked in and was confronted by a burly man who addressed me in a strange accent. I had scarcely heard an American accent before. He told me in a booming voice that his name was Manning Pike, and invited me to sit down and tell him about myself.[3] The interview was very pleasant. I warmed to him and, it seemed, he to me. He listened and then told me what the job was all about. He had taken on the task of printing a number of editions of a book. For reasons that were not very clear, the author had decided to pay privately for having the book printed. When I asked why I was told that there was a suspicion that it would not be welcomed in political circles. I became intrigued. 'Does it tell state secrets?' I asked. Pike guffawed. 'Not in the sense you mean,' he smiled 'but there are those in government who don't

---

[3] Roy Manning Pike was born in Lake City, Minnesota, USA in 1879. He moved to England and studied interior design at the Birmingham Municipal School of Arts and Crafts in 1906-8. In 1911 he moved to ample premises at 2 Riverside, Chiswick Mall, which backs onto the River Thames. In December 1911 he formed a company that manufactured bronze spirit lamps to his design. He married Gwendoline Kate Lewis in 1912 and they had three children, in 1914, 1919 and 1920. At the outbreak of war the demand for spirit lamps evaporated and the company closed down at the end of 1914. He joined a company in Acton making metal components for the war effort. He designed a plaque for presentation to the next-of-kin of service personnel killed in action and set up a factory. But in 1922 it was closed. (Source: Peter Wood, 'In Search of the Elusive Manning Pike,' *Journal of the T. E. Lawrence Society,* **14**(1), April 2004, pp. 61-73.)

Impressions of War

like the idea of the book, even though they don't yet know what's in it.' 'Can you tell me who the author is,' I asked. Again he smiled: 'All in good time, let's see if you and I suit each other first.'

He showed me his press. It didn't take long. The small shop, which had consisted of two rooms back to back, had had part of the dividing wall removed. He had installed a printing machine, a small hand-fed Victoria platen, which at most could take two pages at a time. I told him that it would be a very slow process and, depending on the number of copies required, it could take a very long time.

'Wouldn't it be better to have a large cylinder machine?' I asked. 'Book work these days is usually done on those, they're automatically fed, they take a number of pages on one large sheet and they are all done in one operation.'

He told me not to think in terms of a commercial operation. 'The author could have gone to one of the big printing houses if he'd wanted it done that way,' he said. 'This is going to be a special work. He wants the print to be in the old style and on deckle-edged paper. Famous artists will be engaged to do frescoes and wood-cuts. The bookbinding will be a work of art in itself. Now, Hodgson, are you interested and do you think you're up to it?'

By this time nothing would have made me say no to either question. Here was an opportunity to do something of real worth. We agreed that I would start the following Monday morning on a three-week probationary period. I cycled home knowing that I'd got the chance of a job which, bearing in mind the uncertainty of work at the time, was as near permanent as I could hope.

Pike greeted me very affably on Monday morning and told me how much he was looking forward to our association. He felt that my experience in print would help him enormously in the job he had undertaken. I asked him to explain exactly how it was all going to work. All we had in the shop was the small platen machine, an Albion hand press and two composing frames.[4] Could he tell me

---

[4] The first Albion press was first produced in about 1820 by the firm of R. W. Cope. The name Albion was used to describe a make and style of press that lasted well into the twentieth century.

Pillars of Wisdom

more about the book and its author and what was Mr Pike's job exactly? The smile I got in return was something I was to get very used to. There had been another question in my mind that I refrained from asking. I wanted to know all about Mr Pike himself. An American in London setting up a small private printing press was not an everyday occurrence. Pike first told me about the book. It was the memoirs of a Colonel T. E. Lawrence who had spent the war years helping the Arabs in their revolt against the Turks. The Turks had sided with Germany and the Arab revolt helped the Allied cause. As he was talking I could feel the excitement rise within me. He didn't need to say: 'By the way Hodgson, Colonel Lawrence is Lawrence of Arabia.' I'd already guessed.

The author was paying for the cost of printing the book and it was hoped that one hundred copies would be made.[5] Seeking anonymity, Colonel Lawrence had changed his name and had re-enlisted in the Royal Armoured Corps, under the name of T. E. Shaw.[6] We were to refer to him as Mr Shaw. He was then based in camp in Dorset but would make trips up to London as often as he could. The change of name, plus what Pike had told me at our first meeting about official sensitivity to the book, made it all sound very mysterious. Pike himself was nervous about the project and told me so. He was conscious of having a great responsibility, not only in managing everything in connection with the printing of the book, a mammoth task for one man anyway, but in the wider sense of it being uncensored and liable to meet official disfavour. As far as the practicalities of printing and publication were concerned, Pike had some knowledge of typesetting and had enrolled at the London School of Printing for a couple of terms to increase his experience. He was not a tradesman. All the typesetting was to be in monotype

---

[5] In fact, 211 complete copies were printed.

[6] The full story is even more complicated. In 1922 Lawrence enlisted under the name J. H. Ross in the Royal Air Force. Forced to leave in 1923, he then joined the Royal Armoured Corps as T. E. Shaw. He successfully petitioned to transfer to the Royal Air Force in August 1925.

Impressions of War

and prepared by one of the best firms in London, but Pike could do the corrections and paging up of the forms of type. The printing was to be carried out under his personal supervision at Westbourne Terrace. That was where I came in. I was to be the printer.

Lawrence of Arabia at Aqaba, 1917

As the proofs were printed they would have to be sent to the author to check. If he required any amendments or corrections the process would have to be repeated. A number of artists, engravers and sculptors were being commissioned and their work would be incorporated in the finished work. I began to see the enormity of the task Pike had undertaken. He had no assistance in the administration and managing of the enterprise. No wonder he was worried. I promised to do all I could to ensure success but I couldn't help wondering how long it was all expected to take. When I asked him he simply said: 'It will be finished when it's finished.'

He gave no clue about his own personal background. He had some typesetting already prepared and I got ready to start work on the platen. The first thing I noticed was that it was so old-fashioned it had no motive power and had to be treadled by foot. I pointed out to

Pillars of Wisdom

Pike that the job was going to take even longer unless we could do something about that. He promised to get a motor fixed, which he did in time, but those first few weeks were a nightmare. I was cycling to work from Peckham, a distance of about ten miles, and after treadling that machine all day and cycling home at night my legs were like jelly. I had asked why he had given the impression to my union that there was only about three weeks work. The reply was simple. He would know in that time whether the chap they sent was good enough for the job or not. If not, then he would be out. The three weeks went quickly and Pike declared himself very satisfied with my work. He shook my hand warmly.

My working life settled into a routine. I was often alone because Pike spent a great deal of time out, usually on business but sometimes, as he would tell me in that drawl of his: 'To give myself time to think.' I learned that he lived in Hampstead and would often walk or sit on the Heath, just thinking and worrying about the job. I learned also that he was married to an Englishwoman. She visited the shop during the first week I was there and he introduced us. She was very sweet and charming. The next time I met her in rather embarrassing circumstances. It was during the period before the motor was fixed to the platen machine and we were enjoying some very hot weather. Treadling that machine in my overalls made me sweat somewhat. Pike had said he wouldn't be in until late in the day so I slipped off my overalls and sat treadling in my 'long johns'. Suddenly the door opened and in walked Mr and Mrs Pike. 'Well, well, Hodgson,' drawled Pike. 'What's all this?' I grabbed my overalls and ran for the toilet. We all laughed about it afterwards.

After about three months the final proofs were passed and we could start printing the book. After sending the proofs back the author sent a letter saying he would like to pay us a visit. I was excited at the prospect of meeting him. Lawrence of Arabia was a living legend. The name conjured up mind-pictures of a dashing soldier of fortune, handsome and fearless, dressed in romantic Arab costume, riding hell-for-leather across sand dunes brandishing a sword and exhorting his followers to ever more daring feats of bravery against the cowardly Turks. The very name Arabia was

Impressions of War

romantic enough. To the ordinary person like me it was an exotic and mysterious land where all the women were beautiful and the men looked like Rudolf Valentino. The idea of a quiet Englishman arriving in their midst, being taken to their hearts and leading them to a great victory had captured the British public imagination. Not that we were surprised. Weren't Englishmen looked up to by every other race on Earth anyway?

What I and many others couldn't understand was why Lawrence wasn't very popular with the Establishment figures at home. We put it down to jealousy particularly on the part of the military who perhaps thought that Lawrence didn't deserve the public adulation which he got. They may have been right. Important as they were, Lawrence's efforts against the Turks had not exactly won the war. Having spent so much time on the Western Front I could see this point of view. It seemed that it was a combination of official antipathy and public adulation that led Lawrence to bury himself in the armed forces under an assumed name. The antipathy disappointed him and the adulation embarrassed him. I think he genuinely believed that the suffering and hardship of the Arabs under the Turks and their courageous uprising had not had the recognition they deserved. The publication of his memoirs would, in his opinion, set the record straight.

Came the day when Lawrence arrived at the little shop in Westbourne Terrace. I had no prior idea what he looked like but imagined him to be a tall man of military bearing like my old regimental colonel. His arrival outside was a surprise in itself. There was a sudden roar of a motor cycle coming down the street. The noise stopped outside our premises and a few seconds later a short man of slight build walked in. 'Hello,' he said, 'My name's Shaw. You must be Hodgson?' He spoke quietly in a cultured voice and looked fit and tanned. He was wearing a private's uniform with a brightly-coloured scarf and goggles around his neck. Lawrence, or Shaw as he called himself, looked nothing like the person I'd imagined him to be. It was almost lunch time and when Manning Pike asked him what he would like to do for lunch, he asked in return what we did. We told him that lunch for us was usually some cheese, biscuits, tomatoes and a mug of tea. He said that would do him fine and the three of us sat down around the upturned box which served as our table. He repeated that the simple fare suited him fine. I was getting more surprised by the minute. Over lunch we talked about the book, and again I was surprised at his knowledge of printing. He could discuss in some detail the finer aspects and quality of good craftsmanship in book work, printing inks, paper and printing machinery. He had an appreciation and considerable knowledge also of art and its application in his book. He mentioned the names of artists who were being appointed. I warmed to him and began to feel that here was a man to respect.

He questioned me thoroughly on my background in print. I answered him honestly and said that I had never tackled anything like this before. He smiled at that. 'Neither have I,' he said. I told him that this was my first experience of working in a private press. I didn't like to mention the absence of older men to whom one could turn for guidance but it was on my mind. I felt fairly confident that I could produce work of the right standard, but in the presence of Lawrence himself and seeing at firsthand what the book meant to him, I had a few nerves. He must have read my thoughts. 'The three of us are all in the same boat, Hodgson,' he said. 'I've never written and published a book before, Pike has never produced one and you've never printed one. We'll sink or swim together.'

Something else had become noticeable to me in the few months I'd worked there. My experience up to that point had been in large firms where there was discipline and order. You clocked in at a certain time in the morning and clocked off at night. Meal breaks during the day were scrupulously controlled. Supervision was tight and at times severe. Now I was working in a completely different environment. For a start, there was no clocking in and off. Because he was often out, Manning Pike gave me a front door key. I was put on trust. I could come and go as I liked. It was surprising what effect that had on me. I was more conscious than ever of the need to get in on time, produce a good day's work and not leave before time. It didn't change my political views and I still paid my union dues, but I began to see industry in a different light.

Impressions of War

At last we got down to the actual printing. Mr Shaw had decided on the name *The Seven Pillars of Wisdom* – a Biblical quotation.[7] The book format was designed by Eric Kennington, a well-known artist and sculptor. He was an old friend of the author and had visited Arabia with him after the war. He spent two years there and sketched and painted all the Arab Sheiks who had fought in the revolt. Mr Shaw told me that a great deal of tact and diplomacy had to be used. The Sheiks were not used to anyone making sketches of them and he was afraid that at any moment they might draw their swords from their scabbards! Back in England the sketches and paintings were reproduced by a printing firm in Chiswick and Peckham using the Collophont litho process. Eric Kennington did a number of woodcuts, pictures cut by hand out of boxwood imported from China. Other artists who contributed were Augustus John, Paul Nash, Blair Hughes-Stanton and his wife who was well known under her own name Gertrude Hermes. They were all frequent visitors to the press and always interested in the progress we were making, particularly our reproduction of their own work.

The printing was slow and tedious but utterly absorbing. The paper was very expensive, hand-made rag paper, very hard, rough in texture and deckle-edged. The only way to get beautiful rich printing of type or woodcuts from such paper is to damp it first. This softens the cotton fibres and the result is a soft clear print. Used dry the paper requires more printing ink and heavier impressions into the surface. In the case of fine-line woodcuts particularly, dry paper results in too blodgy and harsh an appearance, certainly to a connoisseur of good printing. Pike and I experimented for some time before we found a satisfactory way to dampen the paper. Too little

---

[7] It comes from the *Book of Proverbs* 9:1 where Wisdom is personified as a good woman enlightening humankind: 'Wisdom hath builded a house: she hath hewn out her seven pillars. Give instruction to the wise man, and he will yet be wiser: teach a just man, and he will increase in learning.' During the Arab Revolt of 1917–18, Lawrence based his operations for a while, in Wadi Rum (in modern Jordan). One of the spectacular rock formations in the area was named by Lawrence 'The Seven Pillars of Wisdom.'

dampness produced the blodgy effect but too much made the paper disintegrate.[8]

Eventually we found the answer, a trough filled with water and a supply of cheaper ordinary cream woven printing paper cut to a size two or three inches bigger all round than the deckle-edged. We dipped one of these in the water, soaked it well and then placed it on a coconut board. Three sheets of deckle-edged paper were then placed on this and the process repeated until we had a big pile of damp and dry sheets together. We then covered the pile with a damp cloth and left it for a few hours. When the water had soaked through uniformly we separated the pile and rebuilt it but this time using one deckle-edged to one ordinary piece of paper Again the pile was left for a few hours. Only in this way, slow as it was, could we ensure that there was sufficient dampness in the deckle-edged paper to take the printing. I had to work very slowly on the machine as all stiffness had disappeared from the paper and it was liable to give as it was placed on the machine. Once the first side was printed, the process had to be repeated for the reverse or backing-up side. After this each sheet was hung up to dry and then put in the hand press to iron out any creases.

The dampening of the paper for the woodcuts followed the same process but the preparation for printing woodcuts was very intricate. The making of a woodcut calls for considerable skill on the part of the artist; it is a sculpture in wood and painted in many colours. Each artist would require certain details in each woodcut to be highlighted. There is far more printing skill required in woodcut work than in say half-tone blocks used in magazines and the like. We had to submit

---

[8] Manning Pike wrote: 'Dampened paper is a trial; kept too long damp it mildews, it changes size, it is difficult to lay on; but fine paper demands it. Moulds of various colours stared up at me one Monday morning when I took the waterproof cover off my stock of paper. Charming and interesting as they were ... I decided that the adornment of the book must be left to the artists. Boric acid was the cure added to the damping water and copper sulphate a better.' (From 'Notes on Printing *Seven Pillars of Wisdom*', *Journal of the T. E. Lawrence Society*, **14**(1), Autumn 2004, p. 57.)

Impressions of War

proofs of all woodcuts to the artists and the author. As the printing of the woodcuts was to be done on paper on which we had already printed text this meant dampening the paper again. Some of the engravings had varying degrees of light and dark shades which meant that overlays had to be cut to suit each one. To do this each woodcut was first proofed three times on rather thick smooth ordinary paper. On the first sheet the lightest parts were cut out. On the second the solid or very dark parts were cut out. These were pasted on the solid or dark parts of the first sheet. The lightest and medium shades were then cut out of the third sheet and what was left of the sheet was pasted on the first sheet. The whole thing constituted a three-ply overlay. The secret was in the pasting which had to be exactly right on the packing or dressing. The overlay was then pasted in position on the platen machine beneath the sheet of paper to be printed and exactly where the impression of the engraved block would come. The small coloured plate or decoration in the front part of the block was printed in three colours.

My worry to make sure the printing was as good as possible was nothing compared with the torment which Manning Pike endured. As I have said, his responsibility was pretty considerable, being in charge of everything, and he took it very seriously. Apart from the everyday worries of administration, suppliers, tradesmen, rent, lighting, bills to pay etc. there was potentially something far more serious. Ever present in his mind was the knowledge that the book was not being censored and it was disfavoured in official circles. I think that in his more depressed moments he imagined himself going to prison, or even being locked up in the Tower of London! These days when our right to freedom of speech has become more established, it is difficult to understand such fears. In the hierarchal social structure of those days, however, such worries were very real.

I never found out Pike's full story. He had come over from America after the war to 'further his interest in printing', having had some experience of print in Minnesota. He had been introduced to Lawrence by Eric Kennington. He was reticent about his family background but he did tell me that his grandmother was of Red Indian blood. He had a mass of black hair and very bushy eyebrows.

Pillars of Wisdom

Once we went for a swim in Paddington Baths and I was surprised at the amount of hair on his body. We must have looked an incongruous pair standing on the top diving board, me being so slim and fair.

T. E. Lawrence in 1915

Pike would pace up and down the little shop in Westbourne Terrace, full of foreboding as to what might become of him and with a wild look on his face. Once he turned to me and said 'Well, Hodgson, can you figure out the best way to commit suicide?' I told him not to talk like that but it did nothing to cure his depression. He continued his wild-eyed pacing up and down. I kept my eye on a couple of spanners on my machine, just in case things got out of hand. He calmed down eventually. When rational, Manning Pike was a charming and likeable man. On a later occasion he said: 'Oh well, Hodgson, I guess there are a couple of bullets in that there revolver

Impressions of War

behind the Albion hand press.' He'd brought in the revolver in case 'we get any trouble from anyone.' I had not even inspected it and had no idea it might be loaded. As soon as he went out I picked it up. Sure enough it was fully loaded! I ejected the bullets and threw them in the Thames as I cycled home that night.

One day when Pike was out, a local police constable on his beat put his head round the door, said 'Good morning' and asked me what I was printing. I showed him a few sheets and explained the process. He told me he was new on the beat and was just making a routine call. Manning Pike nearly had a fit of apoplexy when I told him. In his state of mind, a visit from the police could only mean one thing. When nothing happened as a result of the visit he calmed down.

Whenever we were expecting Mr Shaw I made Pike concentrate on the work in hand to take his mind off his worries. We would go through the whole situation so that Shaw could have an up-to-date report and be shown the work already done. I certainly didn't want Pike pacing up and down in one of his moods when the Brough Superior motorcycle roared to a standstill outside the shop.[9]

One morning it was raining very heavily and I got drenched on my bike ride from Peckham. It was during one of our quiet periods and there was little work to do. I lit a fire in the inner room and boiled up some water. We had a hip-bath in the shop and I poured the boiling water in that, stripped right off, hung my clothes in front of the fire and jumped in the bath. I didn't want to catch a cold. I caught one alright, but in another way. I was standing in the hip-bath in my birthday suit when suddenly the front door opened and I heard Manning Pike say: 'Well, folks, come in and I'll introduce you to my pressman.' He and his visitors entered the shop. Not seeing me in the front area, Pike strode across to the inner room, followed by the others. I had no time to do anything but stand there. Luckily the visitors were two men. What a surprise they got – Pike's pressman naked in front of them surrounded by steaming clothes. We all had a

---

[9] Regarded as the 'Rolls-Royce of motorcycles,' they were manufactured from 1919 to 1940 at the Brough Superior works in Nottingham. 3048 were made, about a third of which are reportedly preserved today by collectors.

laugh about it afterwards. Because of his striking appearance, Pike became a familiar figure in that part of Paddington, and of course it was no secret that we were printing something. Whenever he came striding down the street small boys would shout: 'What ho, Caxton!'

As time went on I got to know Mr Shaw better. He was a quiet charming man and a good raconteur. I learned that he had been educated at Jesus College, Oxford and had won a scholarship to go to Syria in 1910. He did archaeological work in the Middle East and studied and lived among the Arabs, even dressing in Arab clothes. At the outbreak of war he was engaged by the War Office on geographical work and sent to Egypt. The Foreign Office felt that Shaw, or Lawrence as he then was, with his knowledge of the Arabs, could help to organise resistance to the Turkish occupation of the region.[10] He was sent into Arabia and history was made. His first draft of *The Seven Pillars of Wisdom* had been lost or stolen in Reading railway station. He had re-written it from memory.[11]

---

[10] In 1914 the Ottoman (Turkish) Empire stretched from the Black Sea to the Red Sea.

[11] Hodgson mistakenly reported in his original text that the manuscript had been lost in Paddington Station. After rewriting the book, Lawrence decided to circulate his draft among friends and literary critics for their feedback. In 1922 he had it typeset at the printing works of the *Oxford Times* newspaper. To prevent the printers there assembling the book, he sent the chapters in random order. Eight sets of the chapters were printed on a proofing press. They contained numerous errors. The volumes were large and the text was printed in double columns. Six copies remain extant. The readers of this proof edition included George Bernard Shaw, E. M. Forster, Thomas Hardy, Rudyard Kipling and Siegfried Sassoon. In his own copy Lawrence made amendments in response to readers' comments. In May 2001 a collector paid nearly a million dollars for it, at Christies in New York. Lawrence abridged and made further changes to the text for the Pike-Hodgson subscribers' edition. In his Preface to the *Seven Pillars* Lawrence explained that the changes were largely to condense and improve the style, but significant cuts in the narrative were also made. The text of the 1926 subscribers' edition amounts to 250,579 words. The foremost scholar of Lawrence, Jeremy Wilson ('*Seven Pillars* – Triumph and Tragedy', *Journal*

Impressions of War

He was open about the financing of the book, telling us that all his savings were going into it and that he had friends who had promised him financial help. I didn't like to ask him why he had re-enlisted, and especially in the ranks. But I got an impression that civilian life did not appeal to him. I presumed that after ten years in Arab countries, with all their apparent glamour, life in England would be dull. As for being in the ranks, I think he preferred a simple military life without responsibility. It gave him time to indulge in his favourite pastimes of reading, writing and studying the arts. He hinted that his superiors preferred it that way and he was not asked to carry out many of the duties of normal soldiering.

T. E. Lawrence on his Brough Superior Motorcycle, 1927

---

of the T. E. Lawrence Society, **14**(1), Autumn 2004, pp. 9-54) argues persuasively that Lawrence's depressed state of mind, and the financial pressure to finish the job, marred the 1926 abridgement and excluded much material of interest from the work. Many other minor changes were made simply to prettify the alignment of the text on the page.

Pillars of Wisdom

Whenever he came to see us, we would spread out the biscuits and cheese. There were times when he would disappear round the corner and come back with a slab of chocolate. He'd refuse all our food and eat all the chocolate, saying that it would keep him going for a couple of days. He explained that in the desert he'd got used to meagre rations and would sometimes go without food for days on end. It kept him fit, he said. In one camel ride in the desert in a temperature of 120 degrees he had been able to outride the Arabs. He was a very generous man. At Christmas time in 1923, our first year of association, he gave me ten pounds and apologised for not being able to make it more.[12] I was astonished. I had never had a Christmas box before and here was an employer, having given me nearly three weeks wages, saying he was sorry. The gesture was repeated each succeeding Christmas.

When we were three-quarters of the way through printing we moved from Westbourne Terrace to Shepherds Bush. For me this was not very good news as it meant an even longer cycle ride to and from work, but by then nothing would have stopped me seeing the job through. The three days it took to dismantle our plant, pack up everything and install it in our new premises made a change from printing, but we were soon back at it. The printing of the book was finished a few months later. The last job was the decorated end-paper woodcuts which, because of their size, I printed on the Albion hand press. They were too big for our small platen. It was a very slow process indeed. The author was due to visit the following day and we worked late that night in order to be able to report to him that the printing was done. I remember it was exactly 10.30pm when we finished the last sheet. Pike and I looked at each other and shook hands. There was a look of relief on his face. We packed up and went and had a beer to celebrate. I got home after midnight that night.

---

[12] Ten pounds in 1923 is equivalent to about £425 in 2010 prices. And Lawrence was not a rich man.

The Hodgson-Pike 1926 Edition of *The Seven Pillars of Wisdom*

Pillars of Wisdom

When we had received the coloured plates and maps which were printed elsewhere, Mr Shaw paid us another visit to help us gather and collate each section to make up one hundred or so books, so that they could be sent to the bookbinders. Each copy was bound differently. I remember Shaw saying at the time: 'We'll have a joke with my friends and the other people who will be having copies.' Where a certain colour plate depicting an Arab sheik would be put in between pages ten and eleven in one copy, in another copy the same plate was put in between pages sixteen and seventeen and so on. He said it would amuse him to imagine them arguing over it.

So that was the finish of the book. We all shook hands and Manning Pike and I wished the author every success with the volume. Each book had over seven hundred pages of text, woodcut decoration, and colour plates and maps. The cost of production was £90 per copy – a fortune then. I was told that this almost broke Mr Shaw.[13] He thanked us warmly for our part in the production and later presented us with a signed copy each. It was 1926. The three weeks of possible work in 1923 had stretched to three years and had given me a satisfaction and enjoyment that I had not experienced at work before.

My outlook on life had begun to change. I was still the passive radical and impatient to see change in the social structure, but I had seen in the three years a side of industry totally different from what I'd come to consider as the norm. A man didn't have to be swallowed up inside a giant factory, a nonentity whose presence was hardly noticed and whose work consisted of dreary repetition. Not all employers were greedy capitalists bent on exploiting those who worked for them. There could be humanity and enjoyment at work.

---

[13] This cost per copy – equivalent to about £3900 in 2010 prices – was three times the thirty guineas each subscriber had paid, and Lawrence faced bankruptcy. Because of these adverse financial circumstances he published a further abridged version: *The Revolt in the Desert.* (See Robert Graves (1934) *Lawrence and the Arabs,* London: Jonathan Cape, and Jeremy Wilson (1989) *Lawrence of Arabia: The Authorised Biography of T. E. Lawrence,* London: Heinemann.)

Impressions of War

I remember my anxiety as the General Strike loomed.[14] I knew that there was no way that I could avoid taking part in it. It was the British labour movement rising up, not just in support of the miners, but to finally throw off the chains of oppression. Yet I knew, equally well, that I couldn't let down Pike and Shaw. I told Pike about my worries. 'I don't know why you're worried,' he said. 'You only have one choice. With your beliefs and background you have to support the strike.' Such a response made me even more unsettled. If Pike had tried to dissuade me from striking it would have stiffened my resolve to strike but his understanding of my predicament was a complete surprise. My relief when the strike petered out after a couple of weeks is impossible to describe. On the one hand a feeling of bitterness that the battle had not been won, but on the other a sense of joy that I could after all see the job, so nearly complete, finally through.

I never met Lawrence of Arabia again. There have been books written about him that portray him unfavourably, some stressing his homosexuality. I can only speak as I find. I once read that both George Bernard Shaw and Winston Churchill said that when meeting Lawrence they felt they were in the presence of genius. I can't claim to have had the same feeling but I do know that he was a very warm and likeable human being. I couldn't have met a nicer chap and I felt a better person for having known him. I felt privileged to have been of help in printing his book.

---

[14] The General Strike of May 1926 was called by the Trades Union Congress in support of the coal miners and lasted ten days. At its height it involved less than two million workers.

4. How Green Was My Valley

Manning Pike and I suffered a feeling of anti-climax after the *Seven Pillars* was finished. Pike though was optimistic about the future. He was sure that as the fame of the book spread there would be considerable interest in the standard and quality of the artwork and printing. This would lead to orders being placed with us to produce more of the same high-quality work. He said he would go on employing me and I stayed with him. But the orders did not materialise. After two or three months I thought it only fair to him to try to find another job. It was 1926 and work was scarce. I went back to jobbing. Pike and I parted on very amicable terms. 'We'll meet again, Hodgson,' he drawled as we shook hands, a statement that came true some years later.

Meanwhile those subscriber editions of the *Seven Pillars* were becoming famous and beginning to change hands for large sums of money. Out of the blue one day I received a letter from Bumpus the West End bookseller, offering me 100 guineas for my copy.[1] I'd never had so much money. I struggled with my conscience. The book had been a present from Lawrence and I felt I shouldn't part with it. Then I remembered that when giving it to me he had said he would have preferred to give me a present of money but couldn't afford it. The cost of printing and publication had used up all his cash. I was free to do what I liked with it. I was 33 years of age, a married man with two small children and with no security of job or finance. There was really only one choice. For the sake of my family I decided to sell. Mr J. G. Wilson was the manager at Bumpus, a charming Scot. He was very interested in the process of how the *Seven Pillars* was produced and we had a long chat. It was to be a fortuitous meeting.

I decided to use part of my cheque from Bumpus on a summer holiday, something we'd never had before. There was great

---

[1] About £4350 in 2010 prices.

Impressions of War

excitement in our house. We settled on Swanage in Dorset. It was far enough away to make the journey an adventure; it was by the sea and sounded quaint enough. We were the envy of our street at the time. The week at Swanage was a great success.

In 1926 my mother was diagnosed with cancer and she died in February 1927 aged 71, much mourned by us all and particularly my father. He had retired on a state pension of ten shillings a week in 1925 and a union pension of five shillings. At that time Becky received confirmation that another baby was on the way.

In April 1927 I got another letter from Mr Wilson of Bumpus asking me to go and see him. He had got something to tell me that I might find interesting. He introduced me to Robert Maynard, an artist and expert in typography, and told me that Maynard was the Controller of the Gregynog Press. The firm was situated in North Wales and was looking for a pressman. Wilson had recommended me! I had heard of the Gregynog of course. My interest in working in small private printing presses had been fuelled by my experience on the *Seven Pillars*. There were a number, the Golden Cockerel, the Ashendene and the Kelmscott among them. I had given scant thought to Gregynog as it seemed so far away. Yet here I was sitting with the Controller of the Press having been recommended to him.

Maynard invited me to discuss the proposal with him over some tea in a nearby restaurant. He told me that Gregynog (which, he was careful to explain, was pronounced *Gree-gun-ogg* with the emphasis on the second syllable) was situated in a little village called Tregynon tucked away in the hills of Montgomeryshire, about thirty miles from Shrewsbury. I had heard of Shrewsbury, but Tregynon, Bettws Cedewain, Newtown, and Welshpool might have been in a foreign country for all that the names meant to me.

Maynard wanted me for the job. I must admit to being flattered but secretly I didn't fancy Wales very much. Not that I knew anything about it, it just seemed so far away. I told Maynard I would think about it but I wasn't very keen. I was a married man with two children and with another on the way and I would have to discuss it with my wife. He quite understood but suggested I try it for a month on my own to see what I thought.

How Green Was My Valley

I discussed it with Becky. She realised very quickly that I was torn between two desires, to at least give it the month's trial but not to upset her in any way particularly in her condition. As always, her support was unstinting. 'We'll have a shot at it,' she said. 'I'll manage for the month you are away.' So a week or so later I caught the Aberystwyth train from Paddington at three minutes past eleven in the morning, a train I and my family got to know quite well in the next few years. I arrived at Newtown station, 176 miles from London, in the late afternoon, the longest journey I had ever made for a printing job.

Maynard had told me that I would be met at the station and taken to some digs he had arranged for me in Tregynon. There was an old four-wheeler horse-drawn cab outside the station and, thinking this was my lift, I approached it. The driver was Welsh and I had to repeat the name Gregynog several times before he seemed to understand. It was probably his first experience of a cockney accent and I'd forgotten everything Maynard had told me about the pronunciation of the name. We took off and were riding around the little town of Newtown for about half an hour during which we had numerous exchanges about my destination. In the end however the driver gave in and drove me back to the station. I got out of the cab feeling even more lost when a uniformed chauffeur approached me and asked if I was 'Mr Hodgson from London?' I said: 'That's me mate.' 'Well, I have a car here to take you to Gregynog Hall. It's six miles out of Newtown.'

The car was a Rolls Royce! What luxury for someone used to penny tram rides or pedalling his bike over the cobbled streets of London. Here I was, purring along through the leafy lanes of Wales with a chauffeur up front. The driver took me to Tregynon and introduced me to the people who ran the little hotel. These were my digs and very comfortable they were. The driver left me with the instruction to report to Gregynog Hall the next morning.

Impressions of War

Gregynog Hall was owned by two spinster millionaires, Misses Gwendoline and Margaret Davies.[2] They had bought it in 1920, their intention being to set up a centre for the arts and crafts. They had been persuaded to include printing. They had appointed Maynard when the Gregynog Press started in 1922.

The family fortune had come from their grandfather David Davies.[3] He had started as a sawyer in Llandinam, not far from Tregynon, and had become a very wealthy man through railway construction and coal mining. After becoming wealthy David Davies built a big house in Llandinam. Because of his support for charitable causes, he is remembered there by a statue erected in his honour.

On the first morning of my arrival I was given directions from the innkeeper and his wife and set off for Gregynog Hall. I carried my overalls and tools in a little case and walked up through the village street. There were one or two people about and I was greeted quite affably, itself a change from the London scene where everybody seemed to be in a tearing hurry first thing in the morning and with no time for pleasantries. Suddenly I had passed the last house and open country lay before me. There were horses, sheep and cows in the fields, birds were singing and the sun was shining. It was like a dream. I thought I'd wake up at any moment. I turned off the road onto a gravelled drive and followed it for about a mile until I rounded a corner and came face to face with the most beautiful house I had ever seen. It appeared at first sight to be half-timbered but in

---

[2] While travelling extensively in Europe before the First World War, Gwendoline (1882-1951) and Margaret (1884-1963) purchased many works by the Impressionists, and their collection was later bequeathed to the National Museum of Wales. During that War they worked as volunteers for the French Red Cross. They also provided asylum in Wales to a number of Belgian artists.

[3] Known as David Davies Llandinam (1818-1890), he was also involved in the industrialisation of the Rhondda Valley and the foundation of the docks at Barry, near where his statue stands today. He served as Liberal Member of Parliament for Cardigan from 1874 until 1885 and Cardiganshire from 1885 until 1886.

fact the rendering had been painted to give that effect. There was a sunken garden in front of it. I paused for a few moments and took it in. This is where I'm going to work? I asked myself. It was a million miles from Paddington and Shepherds Bush!

Gregynog Hall

A young lady appeared and beckoned me over. 'You must be Mr Hodgson,' she said in a lilting accent. 'Please come in.' Robert Maynard showed me round the Press and introduced me to the rest of the staff: Horace Bray his fellow artist, George Fisher the binder, John Jones the existing pressman, Idris Jones the apprentice and two or three young ladies. Later I was introduced to the Misses Davies and Dr Thomas Jones, the Director and Chairman of the Gregynog Press. It all seemed strangely unreal, but the more Maynard explained what was expected of me the more I felt at home. Right from the start I was treated with great courtesy and friendliness.

Gregynog Hall had been built in the nineteenth century on the site of an older house. To one side were the stables and tack rooms which had been converted into a press on the ground floor with the binding department above. The Press was small and with the same machinery we had for the *Seven Pillars*, a hand-fed Victoria platen and an Albion hand press. The work consisted of printing limited editions of

Impressions of War

famous books and anthologies, some of which were in Welsh. I offered up a silent prayer of thanks that I wasn't a compositor; typesetting in English had never appealed to me – but in Welsh! The books were to be illustrated with woodcuts and engravings by Maynard and Bray.

I found the work interesting and as satisfying as the *Seven Pillars*. Handmade 'rag' paper, made from linen, was used. Much ordinary printing and writing paper is made from esparto grass. Prior to my arrival several books had already been printed but I found that no-one had thought of dampening the paper. It is surprising what a difference it makes to the richness, depth of tone and clear sharpness of the printed word. In some cases the sheets had to be soaked more, two interleaves to one damp, particularly if a certain paper was thicker or the woodcut was a very solid illustration. Again care had to be taken not to get the paper too wet or the print would not take properly. Some books at the Press were printed on vellum from Japan, hard to tear and very expensive. There is no need to dampen the vellum, which of course is made from animal skin.

My experience with Manning Pike had taught me a lot more about the art of printing than I could possibly have learned by working in a normal commercial firm. It was very pleasing that my knowledge and acquired expertise greatly impressed Thomas Jones and the others. I received much encouragement from Robert Maynard and a mutual liking grew up between us. I worked on two books that were due to be published later that year. One was the *Life of Saint David* and the other in Welsh – my first experience of printing something that I couldn't read! The month went by very quickly. I wanted to continue but I couldn't be sure what my wife would think.

I had a long chat with Dr Jones. I had learned that he was connected with the government. He was a charming man and a writer. He wrote a book about the Gorbals, the notorious slum area of Glasgow.[4] He asked me to take on the job permanently. I said I

---

[4] Thomas Jones (1870-1955) was educated at the University College of Wales, Aberystwyth, and Glasgow University. He was appointed a lecturer

would like to, but the final decision would have to be made by my wife. I took the London train. Before asking my wife for an answer I went up to union headquarters in Blackfriars. There was not much prospect of a permanent job. Some jobbing work was all I could really hope for. 'If you've got the chance of a permanent job then take it,' was the advice. I put the options to Becky. 'What would you like to do?' she asked. I said I wanted the job and there was no hesitation from her. 'We'll go' she said.

Back in Gregynog I signed a three-year contract. My wages were to be four pounds and ten shillings per week, a big increase on the £3 average for the jobbing work since leaving Manning Pike.[5] My hours were 48 per week plus two weeks paid holiday per year. In August I made a hurried return to London when my second son Bernard was born. He was named after my old friend Bernard Wetherall. My departure to Wales meant leaving my musical activities behind and our growing families had kept Bernard and me from being the bosom pals we had once been. Nevertheless, we vowed to keep in touch. In Wales I took digs with a family in Tregynon. Walter Phillips was the local butcher and he and his wife made me very comfortable.

He told me of an empty house in Bettws Cedewain, about two miles from Tregynon on the Newtown road. Picturesque Bettws was surrounded by hills. It had about a dozen houses, two inns, two shops (one the post office), a working mill, a blacksmith, a tailor's workshop, a cobbler's shop, a wheelwright's shop, a stone church dominating the village, a school, a village hall, a small workshop-garage with one petrol pump and a stone bridge over a river. The mill was worked by water fed into it from the mill pond which was set up on the same level as the church. The two inns, the New Inn and The

---

at Glasgow in 1901. From 1909 to 1910 he was Professor of Economics in Queen's University, Belfast. He returned to Wales in 1910 as Secretary of the Welsh National Campaign against Tuberculosis. In 1912 he was appointed Secretary of the National Health Insurance Commission (Wales). He was transferred to London in 1916 as Assistant Secretary to the Cabinet, later becoming Deputy Secretary.

[5] About £200 and £133 respectively in 2010 prices.

Impressions of War

Talbot, were run by two villagers, one of whom was the wheelwright and the other worked in the mill.

There was a village green bordered by a mill stream and overlooking the green was a pair of semi-detached cottages. Set in a nice garden with porches covered in honeysuckle and roses, one of them was for rent. Mr and Mrs Daniel Hind were the owners. They occupied the other house with their son Arthur, who was the village cobbler. Dan Hind worked as a gardener at Gregynog Hall and his wife was the village postmistress. The empty house looked ideal and I took it straight away at a rent of seven shillings and sixpence per week. Before this I had made one or two trips in to Newtown on the twice-weekly bus service which constituted the only form of public transport in the locality. I wanted to see a little more of the area and try and imagine how Becky would cope with shopping. The two shops in the village sold basic groceries but I knew that she would miss the variety of shopping in South London.

Main Street, Bettws Cedewain

Dai Williams' wheelwright shop is visible alongside the New Inn.
The Hodgson and Hind house can be seen just beyond the hedge on the left.

How Green Was My Valley

Newtown was an attractive little market town. Shopping would never be like the Walworth Road but it would provide a sufficient range of things to suit a growing family. The first item I purchased there was a brand new bike for just under five pounds. I rode it back to Tregynon thinking what a far cry it was from the days of my old boneshaker.

My wife was full of trepidation at the prospect of life in a tiny village yet adapted herself very quickly. The people in the village were very friendly and we never had the feeling of being unwelcome strangers. The ladies went out of their way to offer kindness and support to Becky and our young family. Our landlady Mrs Hind was a tower of strength. One day when Bernard had just begun to walk he wandered out of our house and into hers. He was always in there, being plied with sweets.

Our elder boy Bert became eight just after the move and his sister Lilian was six. Bert had been at school for three years and Lilian just a year. The change for them was dramatic. London schools were big with classes holding up to sixty pupils. In Bettws there was a brick-built school set in a field, with thirty to forty pupils altogether, ranging in age from five to eleven. Three groups sat in a large room and were taught simultaneously by three teachers. The infants were taught in a smaller room. We had tears in the first weeks from them both. They couldn't understand the Welsh accent and couldn't make themselves understood. But the problem quickly disappeared.

Often my wife and I would be completely bewildered during a conversation. A whole sentence would be utterly unintelligible. The staff at Gregynog told me that I was often asked to repeat myself because in part they hadn't understood me and in part they were fascinated by my strange way of speaking. In those days, when radio was still in its infancy, there were many small communities in the British Isles who had little knowledge of life in a big city.

Gone for us were the ways of London, the music halls, the cinemas, the street pedlars, the trams and buses, the markets, the cobbled streets, the pubs, our families and friends. I had my job that I loved, in which I could be absorbed and where I felt part of a creative process. Becky took much longer to feel at home. Happy

Impressions of War

though she was, her heart was still in London. Our house, the first one we'd had on our own, was comfortable enough but, typically in those days, containing the bare necessities. A large living room with an open fire and cooking hob and with a small kitchen-scullery opening off it comprised the ground floor. The kitchen had a sink with a cold tap. A staircase rising from the living room led to three bedrooms above.

There was no bathroom and the toilet was a little outhouse down the garden with a seat and bucket. There were two outhouses side by side, one for the Hind family and one for us. One of my weekly tasks was to empty the bucket into the nearby stream. The house was brick built and rendered, stiflingly hot in summer and like an ice box in the winter.

I purchased a wireless set. When I set it up there was great excitement in the house. Becky and I and Bert and Lily sat fascinated, listening to a talk on some far distant country. Bert wanted to play with a whip and top which we had bought him. He raised the whip and brought it down. On the way it got entangled with the wireless speaker and the whole lot came crashing to the stone floor, broken beyond repair. It took a couple of months to get it replaced.

The community was split in two: you were either church or chapel, conformist or non-conformist. Sunday was the big day. It seemed that everybody dressed up in their best clothes and went to one of the services. Whole farming families would arrive in their pony-driven traps and it was quite a social occasion. With my scepticism about religion I declined to get involved.

But the vicar Mr Badger invited me to a parish church meeting. The main item on the agenda was to decide how to spend a surplus of church money. Various suggestions were made, all concerning some enrichment of the church itself. I listened and said I thought the money would be better spent on replacing the earth closets in the school with modern flush toilets like we had in London. There was a deathly silence. I soon realised that it was felt that I was blaspheming and I was probably a communist to boot. I wasn't invited again and it didn't worry me one bit. But for Becky it was different. She spent all her time in the village and saw the other ladies every day. To not attend either church or chapel would have set her apart and she also felt a spiritual need to attend services. Gentle pressure was put on her to decide between church and chapel. In order to keep everybody happy she attended both, church one Sunday and chapel the next!

I took to getting on my bike each Sunday morning and exploring the countryside. What joy! You could cycle for miles without seeing another vehicle. Everything was so peaceful. I went further afield to places like Lake Vyrnwy (which supplied Liverpool with its water), Rhayader and the lovely Elan Valley. The scenery was breathtaking. Robert Owen, one of the founders of socialism and the co-operative movement, had been born in Montgomeryshire and I visited the cottage in which he had lived.[6]

Although never a serious drinker I was irked because the pubs in Wales were closed on Sundays. Sometimes on a hot Sunday I rode to Chirbury about twelve miles from Bettws and just over the border in Shropshire, so that I could have a pint of ale. As my son Bert got a little older I used to ride out on a Sunday with him on the crossbar.

We got to know the people of the village: Dai Jones the blacksmith, Dai Williams the wheelwright and part-time publican of the New Inn, the Andrew family who ran the post office and whose daughter Evelyn (or Dolly as she was known) taught in the village school, the Bowens who lived in the chapel house next to the chapel whose daughter Florrie taught in the school, Mrs Powell, the headmistress who lived in the school house up by St Bueno's church, the Hinds our landlords and Arthur their son and village cobbler, who was sweet on Dolly Andrew and she on him (they married after her father died), Hywel Jones who ran the garage, Davies the miller who lived in Mill House opposite us, the Evans family in the Old Post Office next to Mill House, Badger the parson who occupied the vicarage near the church, the biggest house in Bettws and the Jones family up at Bettws Hall, the farm just on the outskirts of the village.

---

[6] Robert Owen (1771-1858) was born in Newtown. He was educated there until the age of ten. He worked in a local draper's shop until the age of sixteen and then moved to London.

Impressions of War

There was a church choir, a chapel choir and even a Gregynog Hall choir and what good voices everybody had. It seemed that every Welsh person was born with this gift. Each village held regular musical concerts or Eisteddfods as they called them, and there was great competition among the performers. An Eisteddfod was held in the concert hall in Newtown each year. Schools for miles around competed. Bettws Cedewain always entered its choir in which Bert and Lily were members. They loved this outing.

On Saturday evenings many of the men would come in from the farms and smallholdings to drink and chat at one of the pubs. A refreshing pint after working in the fields used to soothe their voices and at closing time they assembled on the village green and let rip. A lot of them were in the Gregynog choir, sponsored by the Misses Davies. Sometimes my wife and I would hear those marvellous harmonies across the fields as we walked home. Music was one of the few forms of entertainment to be had. Not everybody could afford a wireless and the nearest cinema was in Newtown, six miles away.

Whist drives and dances were held at the village hall. When we first arrived the music for the dances was provided by records played on a wind-up gramophone. Quite often the dancing would have to stop because the gramophone had run down.

I had my mandolin and tenor banjos and I amused myself strumming the latest popular tunes. Arthur Hind and Hywel Jones suggested that I should form a dance band. The blacksmith, Dai Jones, had a brother Jack living in Manafon, a few miles the other side of Tregynon, who became my drummer. May Lewis, who played the violin and came first in the local Eisteddfod year after year, willingly joined. Ethel Evans, who lived opposite our house, was a wonderful pianist and she completed the number. We had a few rehearsals in our house and in 1930 we played our first dance at the Bettws Village Hall, quickly establishing a good reputation.

My 'Venetian Dance Band' became my abiding hobby and we were in great demand at all village dances for miles around. The demands of Ethel Evans' career affected the band but luckily we quickly found a replacement pianist in Mabel Williams. For a while I was able to augment the band with a trumpet and saxophone but the musicians lived in Welshpool, twelve miles away. The dances we played at started at eight o'clock in the evening and usually finished at two in the morning. The late start was necessary because the many people from farms and smallholdings were always late at work and didn't turn up until ten o'clock.[7]

The Venetian Dance Band, circa 1932

May Lewis (violin), Herbert Hodgson (banjo),
Jack Jones (drums) and Mabel Williams (piano).

May Lewis and her mother were very hard-working, running a smallholding on which they looked after a few sheep, three cows, some pigs, poultry and one horse. May was a regular visitor to our house. Once a week we'd have a band practice in the house and run through the latest music scores that I'd obtained from London. My son Bert became fascinated by the violin and asked if he could learn.

---

[7] See *The Venetian Dance Band* by Bernard Hodgson, privately published 2008.

Impressions of War

May was willing to teach him and I purchased a second hand instrument in Newtown. Bert would cycle up to May's place each week for his lesson. Eventually he became proficient enough to enter the village Eisteddfod and win first prize in his category.

With four pounds ten shillings a week I was about the highest paid employed person in the village. Most people there depended on agriculture for their living and many worked on farms. A farm labourer's wage at that time was thirty shillings per week plus free board and lodging. The average wage of the villagers was about two pounds ten shillings per week. I spoke out against what I considered unfair treatment. To my surprise I found few ready listeners and that the majority of the people around were staunch Conservatives! Once I placed a regular order for the *Daily Herald* in Andrew's shop. 'Oh, that will be two *Heralds* in Bettws,' I was told. 'Mr Jones the blacksmith has one every day'. I had many a chat with Dai Jones after that – the only person in Bettws who sympathised with my politics.

On a summer's evening some of the men in the village would go swimming. A few miles from Bettws lies the village of Aberfechan where there is a natural pool in the River Severn, an ideal spot for swimming and paddling. My son Bert and some other boys were with us one night in that place. Reggie Meddings, who worked with Hywel Jones in the garage, brought along a motor cycle inner tube, blew it up and floated out into the deep part of the pool. Reggie couldn't swim and everybody warned him not to go out too far. He fell off. I was the nearest and I swam up to him. But he grabbed me around the neck and pulled me under. I took in a mouthful of water and unable to free myself, I passed out. Two other swimmers managed to reach us. Reggie passed out as well. Clinging to the inner tube they managed to get the pair of us towards a human chain and gradually we were hauled up the river bank. They pumped and massaged us until we started breathing and regained consciousness. It was a near thing. Bert says that when we were first brought out of the river he thought he'd lost his Dad.

In 1930 the country was in the grip of the slump that followed the Wall Street Crash. Luckily I had a regular well-paid job. My three-year contract came up that year. With no hesitation I signed on for another three years, this time at an enhanced weekly wage of four pounds fifteen shillings per week plus sickness pay for a limited period.[8] In June 1930 another son was born to us. We christened him with the Welsh name of David. I now had four children, hardly the time to give up our relative security and return to London.

There were periods when there was nothing to do. I hated being idle. The Misses Davies sponsored regular concerts at Gregynog at which many famous people performed or attended.[9] The Press designed and printed a programme for each concert. The ladies would show the visitors around the Press. Over the years I had the pleasure of meeting Sir Walford Davies, Master of the Kings Musick, Sir Adrian Boult, the famous conductor, the singers Elsie Suddaby and Keith Faulkner, the poet Lascelles Abercrombie and on one occasion the playwright George Bernard Shaw.

In 1930 Maynard and Horace Bray announced that they were leaving Gregynog and returning to London. We were very sorry indeed when they resigned. In addition to being wonderful artists they were both well liked and respected. I felt Maynard's going very personally. I had come to realise what a tremendous contribution he had made to Gregynog. With his artistry and his knowledge of typography he had built up the Press to a very high standard. Bray had also contributed so much. Like Maynard he was so interested and keen in everything he did. I remember that for the two volumes of *The Plays of Euripedes* he visited the British Museum and made sketches of designs from ancient vases to use in his woodcuts.

When I said goodbye to Robert Maynard he took my home address. Later I received a note from him telling me that he and Bray had set up a small press in Harrow Weald in Middlesex. He repeated

---

[8] About £224 a week in 2010 prices.

[9] The Davies sisters eventually founded the Gregynog Festival of Music and Poetry which ran in two main sequences, 1933-38 and 1956-61. The tenor Anthony Rolfe Johnson revived the third sequence of Gregynog Festivals in 1988 and they have continued annually to this day.

his request that I should contact him if and when I returned to London.

The new Controller was William McCance and he was joined by his wife Agnes Miller Parker. Both were noted artists. She was to become known later for her illustrations for Penguin Books and the *Daily Chronicle*. Once she came second in a world contest in Chicago. Apparently she could draw with one hand and engrave with the other at the same time.

In 1930 a man named Alfred Rouse picked up a tramp in his car, bludgeoned him to death and then set fire to the car with the body inside it. The car was identified as being Rouse's and the body, burnt beyond recognition, was assumed at first to be Rouse. It was believed, though never proved, that Rouse was seeking to fabricate his own death. Rouse was discovered and tried. After a trial which made all the national headlines he was found guilty and hung in 1931. I remember that case because fifteen years earlier Rouse had been one of my comrades in France![10]

The birth of our son David was followed eighteen months later by the arrival of a fourth son in December 1931. This baby decided to arrive earlier than expected and I had to cycle two miles out of the village in a blinding snowstorm in the middle of the night to fetch the midwife. We got back just in the nick of time. Such was the kindness always shown to me at Gregynog that at Christmas, shortly after the

---

[10] See the photograph of Rouse on page 35. The car was burned near Northampton. Rouse stood trial in that town in January 1931 and was found guilty of murder. Shortly before his execution, on 10 March 1931 in Bedford Gaol, he confessed to the crime. The case is unusual in legal history because Rouse was convicted of the murder of an unknown man. Rouse had a copious love-life and some argue that this swayed the jury. A chapter in Alan Moore's 1996 novel *Voice of the Fire* tells Rouse's story in first-person narrative, brilliantly portraying the psychological damage wreaked by war. The legal case was dramatised in a 1951 episode entitled 'The Mallet' of Orson Welles' radio drama *The Black Museum*. (Source: http://en.wikipedia.org/wiki/Alfred_Rouse. Accessed 11 June 2010.)

How Green Was My Valley

event, Miss Gwen Davies sent a complete dinner for my whole family, delivered in the Rolls Royce. We decided on the Welsh name Ivor for the new baby.

That year Bert our eldest won a scholarship to Newtown County School. That meant a trip to Newtown to buy him a bike, on which he cycled the six miles each way to school every day. It also meant buying him a smart cap and blazer. Bernard, David and Ivor started at the village school when they were three to four years old.

Every year we were able to afford a trip to London to see family and friends. We stayed either with my sister Elsie in Forest Hill or Becky's sister Li in Bermondsey. We were looked upon as wanderers returning from some far-off land. We used to take the children sight-seeing. Bernard always wore a cap but like so many small boys he insisted on wearing it back to front. Becky and her sister once took Bernard to Selfridges. He wandered away from them and got lost. He was discovered by a shop assistant crying his eyes out and was taken to an office and plied with sweets to console him. He was convinced he'd never see his mother again. What made matters worse was that no-one could understand his accent.

Bert would have had a carefree fortnight playing with his cousins and doing things which were unknown in Bettws – going to the cinema, roller skating, swimming in a proper pool, playing on the swings and roundabouts in the local park, eating fish and chips out of a newspaper, and buying ice cream from the street vendors.

On our annual trips to London I always went to see Mr Wilson of Bumpus. The copies of the subscribers' edition of *The Seven Pillars* were becoming prized possessions and the Gregynog books were gaining in popularity. Wilson and Bumpus capitalised on this by getting me to autograph a few copies while I was in London. For this I was paid two guineas per copy, nearly a half a week's wages to me, but worth £5 or more on the price at which Bumpus sold each copy. I always enjoyed seeing Wilson. He was a charming man and I knew that he placed a regular order for Gregynog books. We always had an enjoyable chat; he was interested in fine printing and would want to know what I was currently working on. He asked me once to write down the story of the *Seven Pillars* and sometime later I received a

Impressions of War

letter from a publication called *The Monotype Recorder* asking my permission for it to be printed in a forthcoming issue. I was paid five guineas for that.

After my 1934 visit to Wilson's office, I walked along Oxford Street and noticed a down-and-out man moving towards me. He had a shaggy beard and shabby clothes. As he drew near a voice drawled: 'Hodgson, I guess?' I stopped in surprise and then recognised him. It was Manning Pike! I was pleased to see him. I remembered how decent he had been to me: now there was a chance to repay his kindness. What took my eye were his boots: the soles were at least two inches thick. I marched him, boots and all, into a nearby restaurant for a meal. He told me things had not been going too well for him in business. While we were waiting for the waitress to serve us I remarked on his footwear. He was so pleased I'd noticed them that without further ado he took them off and placed them on the marble-topped table. He told me that he was going to submit them to the War Office, saying that an army could match in them forever without them wearing out. Then the waitress came along with our meal, saw the boots and let rip. She ordered Pike out of the restaurant but I calmed her down. I never heard the outcome of his submission to the War Office, but I did tell him before we parted that as an old infantryman I wouldn't have fancied going far in them. I never saw Pike again and believe that eventually he returned to America.[11]

---

[11] After printing the *Seven Pillars,* Pike had had difficulty in getting work. In 1929 his wife died. His children had to be looked after by relatives and friends. He sold off his printing equipment and anything else of any value. Eventually he depended on charity. When Hodgson saw him in Oxford Street he was at Rowton House refuge in Hammersmith for down-and-outs. In 1933 Lawrence paid for him to go back to America, but after trying to borrow money from his father and brother he returned to England. His daughter Mary was drowned during the Second World War. Little is known about Pike until 1948 when a photograph taken in Kensington of him and his then girlfriend appeared in the *Picture Post.* Using this, his daughter Jane traced him to a flat in Chelsea. He was still wearing the boots that he had shown Herbert Hodgson in the 1930s. He died in April 1967 and is buried in an unmarked grave in Gunnersbury Cemetery in West London.

How Green Was My Valley

In 1933 I had to decide whether to renew my contract at Gregynog. The country was still in the grip of the slump and millions were unemployed. The advice from my union headquarters was unchanged from six years earlier. I signed a new contract for a further three years. I was enjoying my work at the Press more than ever. Any misgivings after the departure of Maynard and Bray were dispelled by the artistry of the others, particularly Blair Hughes-Stanton and Agnes Miller Parker. Wilson of Bumpus showed me some very complimentary reviews of our books, in which the reproduction of the engravings had attracted attention. One book we printed that year, *The Fables of Esope*, was bound in skin from the sheep which roamed the Kerry hills, a local beauty spot near Newtown, where I often cycled on Sundays.

Under one roof were gathered graphic artists who were encouraged to express themselves in whatever designs they wished to create and the craftsmen who had the skill to reproduce those designs into the reality of finely bound and printed books. The aim of Gregynog was to create a unique and lasting library of beautiful books. Everybody who worked at the Press was dedicated to the task, from the locally-recruited village girls who painted with such care the artist's woodcuts and engravings, George Fisher (probably at that time the finest bookbinder in Britain), printers John Mason, John Jones, Idris Jones and myself, and of course the various artists.

There was another upheaval at Gregynog in 1933 when the McCances and Hughes-Stantons left and an American named Loyd Haberly became the Controller. He was a very nice chap with a great interest in fine printing.

In 1935 I was shocked and saddened when I heard of the death of T. E. Lawrence in a motorcycle accident. I knew that he had a passion for speed on his Brough Superior. He was only 46 years old.[12]

(Source: Peter Wood, 'In Search of the Elusive Manning Pike,' *Journal of the T. E. Lawrence Society,* **14**(1), April 2004, pp. 61-73.)

[12] A fresh burst of publicity after the publication of *Revolt in the Desert* resulted in Lawrence's assignment to a remote base in India in late 1926,

Impressions of War

Idyllic as our life was, a number of things nagged at us. First was our innermost desire to return to London, pent up for so long. Second was the growing restlessness of Bert and Lilian. Our annual trips to London had whetted their appetites for life in a big city compared with the rural simplicity of Bettws. Third was our worry about jobs for them. The only industry for miles around was agriculture. The fact that Bert was leaving school created a sense of urgency. We had to make a decision and we both knew what it would be.

Bert had agreed to coming into print and when I got to London I contacted W. H. Smith and enquired about an apprenticeship. The response seemed to be encouraging but when he went to see them he was shattered to find that he'd been turned down. They had a recent experience of taking on a grammar school boy who, because of his superior education, thought he knew it all and just couldn't be taught. 'We prefer to take on fourteen-year olds who we can mould,' Bert was told. Within a couple of days he got a job in a company making drawing instruments and his departure from Wales was complete.

Bert's departure to London finally decided us. Early in 1936 I approached Miss Gwen Davies and explained the situation to her. She cried at the news but was very understanding and accepted my three months' notice. I wrote to Robert Maynard and enquired about the possibility of employment with him. He replied that he would be delighted to have me.

So ended a period of my life, so different from anything I could have imagined when I first met Maynard in Wilson's office nine years previously. I had settled myself into a tiny community where time seemed to stand still. It was as if I had been looking through a window at a rural scene of Britain as it had been for centuries. The

---

where he remained until the end of 1928. Based for some time in Bridlington in Yorkshire, he continued to serve the RAF until March 1935. His fatal motorcycle accident on 19 May 1935 was near Wareham in Dorset. A dip in the road obstructed his view of two boys on their bicycles; he swerved to avoid them, lost control and was thrown over the handlebars. He died six days later. The spot is marked by a small memorial at the side of the road. The circumstances of his death led to increased, and eventually successful, calls for the compulsory use of motorcycle helmets.

How Green Was My Valley

farm labourer arriving at Dai Jones's smithy with a couple of mammoth carthorses, the forge and anvil, the smell of burning hoof and Dai sweating away in his leather apron. Arthur Hind tapping away in his cobbler's shop talking through a mouthful of tacks. The farm carts delivering crops to the mill, the mill wheel turning, driven by the steady stream of water from the pond above and the murmuring of the millstones grinding out the dirty-looking flour. Dai Williams in his wheelwright's shop surrounded by neatly laid out skeletons of cart wheels of all sizes, gently coaxing them together. My Sunday morning bike rides through such glorious countryside as could be imagined and how it made me happy to be alive.

Above all I remember my days at the Press. The many discussions with various artists on how best to reproduce their work on the printed page, the experiments with colour mixing, the completely absorbing presswork which followed and the feeling of deep satisfaction shared with the artists at the finished result. Altogether I had been involved in the printing of twenty four books with over three hundred woodcuts. I was proud of my name appearing in the books. Without wishing to sound immodest, at 42 I felt a sense of achievement.

The Christmas of 1935 was our last in Bettws. I cannot claim that we were sad. We knew that one day we would return to London and once the decision had been made we were anxious to get away. But we were overcome with the genuineness of the farewells from people at the Press and from the villagers of Bettws. Shortly after we left I received from Miss Gwen Davies a handwritten letter of thanks that I have treasured ever since.

[The following testimonials were added by the editors.]

Extract from a letter from Miss Gwendoline Davies to Herbert Hodgson, dated 25th March 1936:

> We were very sorry to lose you from the Press, but quite understand that with your children growing up it is very

necessary for their future welfare and employment that you should be near a large town.

I should however not like you to leave without sending you our thanks and our appreciation of the splendid work you did for us at the Press and especially for the way you were willing always to help us when there was a rush such as often happened at the last minute before a Conference or a Festival

On 7th April 1954, Thomas Jones read a paper to the Double Crown Club on his time at the Gregynog Press:

Luckily we had a pressman, Herbert John Hodgson, who had printed the *Seven Pillars of Wisdom* for T. E. Lawrence. Hodgson was a Cockney who played a mandolin and tenor banjo and formed a dance band for the entertainment of the surrounding villages. He reproduced with infinite care the fine tones and masses and delicate white lines of Stanton's blocks with complete success, especially in the folios *The Revelation of St John the Divine* and *The Lamentations of Jeremiah*.

Extract from an article in *Printing World*, 23rd May 1974:

Hodgson's work on the finely cut wood blocks of Blair Hughes-Stanton and Fisher's elaborate toolings on the special Levant Morocco bindings were perhaps the high points of the Press achievement.

Extracts from *A History of the Gregynog Press,* by Dorothy A. Harrop, 1980:

Maynard came to be of the opinion that Hodgson was probably the best pressman in the country at that time. ... Hodgson's name appears for the first time in the Colophon and his masterly touch is already apparent. ... The printing of these...... represents a triumph for Hodgson.

The presswork ... appears faultless and was much admired: 'I do not think that I have ever seen such a beautifully printed book, an example of the finest presswork I have seen.'

Much of the success of these was due to Herbert Hodgson's incomparable skill as a printer.

'I do not think that I have ever seen presswork of such uncanny perfection.'

Herbert Hodgson's resignation ... was a sad day for the Press as it was unlikely that a printer of similar stature would be found to replace Hodgson.

Extract from a letter to Bernard Hodgson from Dorothy A. Harrop, 1993:

He was a very great printer. I have such happy memories of the day I visited him. We got on famously ...

Extract from a letter to Bernard Hodgson from David G. Lewis, 1999:

He undoubtedly was, and is remembered today, as one of the great Printers of the twentieth century. Who else could have printed Blair Hughes-Stanton's woodcuts with such amazing clarity, losing none of the detail?

Extract from an address by David Vickers, Controller at Gregynog on 21st June 2008:

Gregynog's craftsmen were responsible for taking certain aspects of book production to new heights: the camaraderie between the pressman Herbert Hodgson and the engravers took the printing and execution of wood engraving to a level rarely equalled. Hodgson, who came to Gregynog fresh from printing the now much sought-after limited edition of T. E. Lawrence's *Seven Pillars of Wisdom* for Manning Pike, was a fine craftsman who had come, through a trade apprenticeship and general printing office experience, to be among the finest printers of the time. He was also a Cockney, and a 'character', and it is this unique combination when having their full scope in perhaps the 'formal' environment of the Gregynog Press which led him to taunt (in the nicest sense) the engraver

Impressions of War

Hughes-Stanton to achieve the unparalleled quality of engraving he did. Hodgson would challenge Stanton with something like: 'There's no engraving you can cut too fine that I can't print.' Stanton would rise to the challenge by engraving finer lines; Hodgson would print them – beautifully. (This was no mean achievement considering the softness of the paper at his disposal, which would thicken any image) The intricate 'make-ready' he cut to get his results are still viewed with awe today; and I feel some link to him as I use his methods to print the engravings in our current books.

London had changed considerably from 1927. Then it had been surrounded by small towns and villages. Now it was difficult to see where London ended. The Underground railway extended in all directions. Factories and shopping parades lined the new roads which had been constructed in and out of the capital. Estates of houses, private and council-owned, were everywhere to be seen. New industries had emerged, particularly in electrical goods, processed food of all kinds, household goods and furniture, cars and motor bikes, aeroplanes, cinemas, wireless, records, cosmetics and so on.

But the country was still divided between rich and poor. There was comparative prosperity in London and the south, but elsewhere the situation was still pretty grim for a lot of people, with high unemployment. 1936 was the year of the famous Jarrow march. Very noticeable was the number of people living in the London area who had emigrated from the worst-affected regions: South Wales, the North, North-East, Scotland and Ireland. Their different accents were to be heard everywhere.

Robert Maynard and Horace Bray had set up in business in Harrow Weald. Harrow Council had built an estate at Pinner and when I applied I was told there was a council house available at 65 Pinner Hill Road. It was a modern semi-detached, three-bedroom house with two rooms, a kitchen and cloakroom downstairs and three

How Green Was My Valley

bedrooms and bathroom upstairs. For the first time we had a bathroom and electric light and power. This was quite a novelty for Lilian and the three younger boys who were forever throwing the switches for the first few days.

Bernard (aged eight) and David (aged five) were duly enrolled in Pinner Council School. Just as Bert and Lilian had suffered the problem of accents when first we moved to Wales it was now the turn of Bernard and David. Bernard can remember being stood up against the wall in the school playground and being made to speak, at which the other boys laughed their heads off. Becky had a few tears to contend with in that first week or so. Bert came to live with us after a few months and after I had asked Maynard if he could join the Press and learn the trade. Maynard consented quite readily although it was not possible for Bert to enter a proper apprenticeship because of his age.

Robert Maynard and Horace Bray had chosen the name Raven Press for their enterprise. Their original intention was to print limited edition bookwork, illustrated by them and to the same quality as that carried out at Gregynog. But Maynard and Bray had found it difficult to make a commercial success of printing books and they had parted company. By the time I joined in March 1936 Bray was no longer there and the Press was concentrating on printing Christmas cards designed by Maynard with wood and lino cuts by him and other artists. Again I had the pleasure of working with Agnes Miller Parker and Gertrude Hermes. There were about a dozen people employed at the Press. I was put in charge of the press shop.

Despite modern development, Pinner retained the atmosphere of a country town. We could walk to the top of Pinner Hill Road and be in open fields. Yet London was only a tube ride away. Becky was overjoyed that she could catch a tube train at nearby Hatch End station and go right through to the Elephant and Castle without changing. From there it was a penny tram ride down the Old Kent Road and she was at her mother and sister Li's house in Marcia Road just around the corner from the Dun Cow public house. She made that trip most weeks. Often at week-ends we would take the family over to visit, or other members of our families would come to us.

Impressions of War

I still felt the order of things needed changing. There was too much unfairness in the way society was structured. One evening a Labour Party canvasser called. I joined. It was a few months after the General Election of 1935 when the Conservatives had been returned. I was asked to go out canvassing, something which didn't appeal to me very much. But as I was now a member of the party I agreed. I was given a bundle of leaflets and allocated an area of Hatch End.

Listening to the wireless had become a remarkable means of entertainment in most homes. To sit in your own armchair and listen to music, drama or talks on current affairs was something that a few years earlier had not even been dreamed about. I particularly enjoyed broadcasts by the well-known dance bands of the day, Jack Hylton, Henry Hall, Jack Payne, Ambrose, many of them coming live from venues that the likes of us were unlikely to attend – The Dorchester Hotel, Grosvenor House and The Savoy. I remember also the BBC 'Music Hall' broadcast every Saturday evening. Comedians such as Clapham and Dwyer, Tommy Trinder and Murgatroyd and Winterbottom (in reality Ronald Frankau and Tommy Handley) appeared regularly as did comediennes Elsie and Doris Waters (performing as 'Gert and Daisy') and Suzette Tarri. My favourite was Billy Bennett, billed as 'almost a gentleman'. He told very funny monologues.

The recording industry had blossomed and the wind-up gramophones with the large speakers were being replaced by electric-powered radiograms, beautifully-finished console models that were pieces of furniture in themselves. We purchased one in Pinner and it was like having a wonder of the world in our living room. We moved the rest of the furniture around to give it pride of place. The advent of talking pictures had seen a boom in film-going, and plush cinemas were springing up everywhere. We had three near us: the Langham in Pinner, the Odeon in Northwood Hills and the Essoldo in Northwood. One night a week at the pictures became a regular feature of life in the majority of households.

During 1936 my father's health deteriorated. He was hospitalised and in October he died of heart failure aged 76.

How Green Was My Valley

That year saw the abdication of Edward VIII. It seemed that he was being forced to go because he was too sympathetic towards the plight of the unemployed and too critical of the Government. This feeling stemmed from a famous photograph of him standing outside the cottage of an unemployed South Wales miner and reportedly saying: 'Something must be done.' But I have long-since realised that my interpretation of his abdication was wrong.

Robert Maynard had a secretary named Alice Badrick. She was a tower of strength in the Press and ran things when Maynard was not there. Suddenly in 1937 another lady appeared in her place. It took us a while to find out that Alice Badrick and Robert Maynard had decided to live together. In those days such an event was shocking enough but in a small company like the Raven Press it was like a bombshell. A few weeks later I was stopped on my way home on my bike by a distraught Mrs Maynard. She pleaded with me to intervene, to speak to her husband and persuade him to go back to her. I have never felt so sad and helpless. I had got to know the Maynards very well during my time at Gregynog and I liked them both. There was no way I could promise to intervene; Maynard and I were not close enough for that.

In 1938 Maynard announced that the Raven Press was moving to Alperton near Wembley. Trade had been looking up and bigger premises were required. A man called Hugh Tregascus was brought in and the business was separated into two, one concentrating on cards and one on printing. In addition to the cards we had a book to print: *Gray's Elegy*. Tregascus wanted me to print it, a task I took on somewhat reluctantly. I had been working on an automatic machine for the cards but now it was back to the platen and hand-feeding.

One consolation was that again I had the pleasure of working with Agnes Miller Parker, who did the woodcuts for the book. Another pressman was bought in. His name was Gray, a lovely chap and a good pressman. He got his leg pulled about having the same name as the author of the *Elegy*. Another printing job I remember that year was a special brochure about farming in Russia. It was illustrated with beautiful photographs of agricultural scenes and commissioned by the government of the USSR.

Impressions of War

Alperton was too far to cycle from Pinner so we moved to 102 Rydal Crescent, Perivale. It was a modern house, bow-windowed, terraced and privately owned. One of London's new roads, the Western Avenue, passed nearby and I marvelled at the fact that cycle tracks had been provided on each side. But the inside of the house was in a very bad state of repair and decoration and the necessary restoration work had only just started when we arrived with the removal van. After weeks of disruption the workmen left. We heaved a sigh of relief but it wasn't the end of our problems. Not long after moving into the house we discovered it was infested with cockroaches. I notified Ealing Council and we were barred from the house while it was fumigated. I thought that we had left behind such dangers when we moved from the poor housing of South London.

Then six-years-old Ivor contracted scarlet fever. It was so severe that he was committed to Clayponds Isolation Hospital in South Ealing with all visitors barred. It was a terrible time particularly for Becky, who became convinced that we were going to lose him, and for Ivor, a small and very frightened little boy who was not allowed visits from any of his family. Apart from peering through a window there was no contact between him and the rest of us for six weeks. I cannot believe that that would be allowed nowadays.

By this time Bert was living with us and working at the Raven Press. He developed two passions, music and a motor bike. The violin was too tame for him and he bought a trumpet. He became quite proficient at it in time and joined a local dance band, in effect taking up where I left off. By the time of our return to London the music scene had changed; the banjo had been replaced with the guitar and my dance band days were finished. Bert's motor bike, a second-hand BSA costing twelve pounds ten shillings, was the undoing of his trumpet playing. He had a spill on it one day and split his lip. So he bought a tenor saxophone, which made a much gentler sound. In time he bought an alto sax and clarinet.

During 1938 there was the threat of another war with Germany. It was unbelievable. The Great War had been the 'war to end all wars' and it was impossible to contemplate another. We carried on living our lives and went away on holiday again, this time to Ramsgate.

How Green Was My Valley

Bernard was packed off for his regular visit to Bettws but this time David, who was eight, was allowed to go with him. In September came the Chamberlain-Hitler meeting and a slump in trade. Printing was so badly hit that the Raven Press had to go on a two-day working week. The slump lasted about five weeks and it proved too much for Bert. He left and started jobbing around just as I had done in the early 1920s. He applied for unemployment pay and received two shillings a day. Each morning he would phone up all the local printing firms and get the odd two or three hours work. He never returned to the Raven Press.

The move to Perivale meant another change of school for the younger boys. Bernard seemed to be doing well both academically and on the sports field. His prowess at cricket that summer came to the attention of the editor of the Lyons sports sheet which was printed on the back of the menu in the J. Lyons teashops. The sports sheet was changed every week and one of its features was the presentation of a Dundee cake to someone who, in the opinion of the editor, had achieved some prodigious feat on the sports or athletic field. Bernard was selected to receive the cake for a week in August after the completion of his school's cricket season. When we were on holiday in Margate, Becky went into a Lyons teashop and asked if she could have one of the menus. After she had explained who she was and had pointed to our three boys with their noses pressed up against the window her request was granted. We stood on the pavement looking at Bernard's name on the back.

Two weeks after our holiday in Margate came the fateful Sunday 3 September 1939, when we heard Chamberlain announce that we were at war with Germany. For months the inevitability of war had been hanging over us. Civil Defence had become a priority and in early 1939 I had trained as an Air Raid Warden.

Bernard had won a scholarship to Greenford County School, newly built and due to open its doors for the first time in early September. During that week we got a letter saying that because of the outbreak of hostilities the opening was being delayed. As far as Bernard was concerned the war meant another four weeks holiday!

5. A People at War

At first there was little change at the Raven Press. We carried on with the printing of cards and had an order to print another book. But Maynard was pessimistic about being able to carry on. 'It all depends on how long the war lasts,' he told us. We weren't as optimistic as in 1914 when the war was going to be over in two weeks but most people thought it wouldn't last more than a few months. Bert was nineteen and was called up straight away. He went into the Royal Army Service Corps, taking his sax and clarinet with him to break the monotony. I was appointed Air Raid Warden for our locality, which meant that every time the siren sounded I went round the streets blowing a whistle and telling everyone to take cover. Not that there was anything to take cover from in those first few weeks.

Work was getting slack at the Raven Press and then out of the blue Robert Maynard told me that he had had a request from Gregynog to loan me back to them to finish a couple of books. He agreed to release me and it was up to me. As always I discussed it with Becky and agreed to go on the basis of returning every weekend and the understanding that should air raids become a problem in London I would return at once. This time I was at Gregynog for two to three months. My presence there was due to Idris Jones, the pressman, having gone into the RAF. Idris had been a compositor originally but had taken over the pressman's job after I had returned to London in 1936. It was like old times. I stayed in the inn in Tregynon and visited people we knew in Bettws.

When I returned to Perivale we set about moving house once more. Becky had felt for some time that the house was too far from the shops. I hadn't appreciated the problem. What man did in those days? She prepared breakfast and packed lunches for Bert, Lilian and me and then breakfast for the three younger boys. The boys came home for lunch and later for tea. After that the three working members of the family came home to a cooked dinner. We had no

A People at War

fridge and no facilities for keeping food, so Becky went shopping every day. The nearest grocery shops were in Greenford, a two-mile bus journey away. We soon found another house to rent: 21 Wedmore Road, Greenford. For the first time we had moved into a semi-detached with a good-size garden.

I decided to pay a visit to Bernard Wetherall who was living at Buckhurst Hill in Essex. I asked young Bernard if he fancied cycling there and back with me, a round trip of about fifty miles in the one day. He was keen and so one Sunday we set off. We reached Buckhurst Hill by lunch time and were entertained very generously by Bernard Wetherall and Marie. After lunch he played the piano and we sat in the garden and reminisced about old times. The journey home took longer than expected and we were pretty tired by the time we reached home. It was a relieved-looking Becky who greeted us.

This was at the time of the 'phoney war' in 1940. The Allied and German armies were facing up to each other in France and Belgium, but no large-scale offensive was taking place. Even so, there were tragedies unfolding in some households. Just before we left Perivale tragedy struck the Cutler house next door to us. Desmond Cutler, aged 21, had volunteered for the army as soon as war had broken out. He was a fine young man and their only child. One day a telegram came from the War Office, Desmond was missing believed killed. I shall never forget the Cutler's faces.

After the evacuation of Dunkirk in 1940, air raids became a nightly occurrence. My three months in Wales had meant losing my warden's post and so I became a 'fire-watcher' both at work and in our street. This meant doing a shift of two hours on most nights. Most of the men in the street shared the fire-watching duties. One was called Ernest Henry. When war was declared he painted the Nazi emblem, a Swastika, on the pavement outside his house explaining that when the German pilots saw it they would think him a Nazi sympathiser and not drop bombs on his house!

I remember the general feeling of hopelessness after Dunkirk. The war in which we thought we would be the victors – after all, we'd beaten the Germans in the previous conflict – had suddenly gone dramatically wrong. The unthinkable had happened: the British

Impressions of War

army had been defeated and swept aside. Even more unbelievable, the Germans were now poised to invade us and they would probably succeed. My socialist leanings were severely stretched by having to admit that Winston Churchill, a Conservative, was just the man we needed at that time. His speeches, about fighting on the beaches and everywhere else, helped to give us hope we would win through. Then the RAF started performing miracles in the skies above us.

We were allocated a corrugated-iron Anderson air raid shelter and it was installed in our garden. A hole approximately 2.50 metres by 2 metres by 1.50 metres deep was dug out, a concrete floor laid in the bottom and 100mm thick concrete walls lined the sides. The superstructure of the two longitudinal sides of the shelter consisted of 2 metre long sheets of corrugated iron with curved ends which were bolted together to form an arch. The ends of the shelter were plain sheets of corrugated iron with an opening at the front for access. The earth from the hole was then backfilled up and around the superstructure. Bunk beds that would sleep four children were supplied. Any other furniture had to be found by the householder. The main drawback was that we had to share the shelter with the family next door: Lou Cordon, his wife, daughter and son. We did that for some months. The air raid sirens would sound about seven-thirty each night and we'd all pile in. Five children would somehow cram themselves into the two bunk beds and we grown-ups squatted on chairs, remaining there until seven the next morning.

At first Lilian crammed in with us. Then she volunteered for the Auxiliary Territorial Service (ATS) and left to do her bit. The air raids grew in intensity, particularly during the Battle of Britain in August and September of 1940. I cannot claim that we experienced anything remotely resembling what others in London were going through. Becky's sister Elizabeth (Li), her family and Becky's mother were forced to leave Marcia Road, Bermondsey when a bomb demolished the back wall of the house. They were in the shelter in the back yard although Li's husband Alf had been inside the house making a tray of tea. He was on his way out with it when the bomb fell. He was lucky to escape injury. They were re-housed in nearby Henshawe Street but were quickly bombed out of there, again

A People at War

without injury, and finished up in Fremantle Street. Real tragedy however struck my family in October when my sister Elsie was killed in an air raid while out shopping in Lewisham High Street one afternoon. She was 48 and left her husband Harry Sims and sons Jimmy and Stanley. During her funeral service at Hither Green Cemetery a German fighter strafed the cemetery and the graveside service was interrupted, but no-one was hurt.

A Bombed London Street

Apart from the danger of falling shrapnel and one of our own anti-aircraft shells once falling on Wedmore Road, the nearest we ever came to disaster was when the pub 'The Load of Hay' was hit by a 'land mine'. It stood just a few hundred metres from us in its own grounds and surrounded by trees. It was completely demolished and the family which ran it all killed. Although they usually slept in the cellar, they had apparently decided to have a change and sleep in their beds. If they had been in the cellar they probably would have survived. I learned later that the so-called 'land mine' was the first dropped in the war. They were huge bombs which descended by parachute and I can remember seeing the remains of the parachutes hanging from the trees around the piles of rubble.

That summer the Raven Press closed and I had to find another job. There was nothing available in print, the industry, like so many others in wartime, had practically stopped. I took a job as a warehouse man in the Co-op store in Hanwell. This was totally different from what I had been accustomed to. I thought it was going to be easy compared with my job as a craftsman in print, but it's an old saying that every man's job looks easy to the other man, until he tries it!

I am not a hefty chap for lifting and stacking provisions. I was to learn from the manager that there is a knack in such work and it does not always require strength. For example sugar was in two hundredweight sacks. I tried lifting one and failed. The best way to move it was to inch it along gradually left to right. I tried stacking cases by piling them on top of each other until I had to struggle and reach very high but was then shown the simple dodge of placing a case on the floor and then standing on it, so raising myself and lessening the lifting strain. One day I had helped to unload a van and I placed three cheeses, each weighing 70 pounds, on a little trolley and started up the ramp into the warehouse. Of course it would happen to me, I reached the top of the ramp and slipped on the wet surface, the lot rolled down again and the cheeses chased each other all over the warehouse yard. Another time I was wheeling cases of butter, with which I had the knack of stacking properly. Suddenly someone shouted 'Look out, mate!' I hadn't noticed that one of the cases had slipped and butter was oozing out on to the wheels. They didn't need greasing for a month.

My experience in the grocery trade lasted about nine months. I didn't really enjoy it. It was very heavy manual work which takes some getting used to when you are nearly fifty years of age and starting it for the first time. Without wishing to sound immodest, I felt a little demeaned by it. I was proud of my craftsmanship in print.

A People at War

And there was the question of money. My wages in print had been five pounds a week. Now at the Co-op I was getting three pounds fifteen shillings. I was overjoyed when my union notified me that there was a vacancy for a pressman at Harrisons, a firm of printers based in Hayes, Middlesex. I applied for the job and got it. It was not like working in a private press, but I was back in print.

Ealing education authorities decided to encourage the evacuation of children. It was all voluntary. Becky and I agreed that we should let the three younger boys go. It was not a decision taken lightly. One day in October 1940 she took them to Greenford County School and watched them boarding coaches and to be driven off. Bert was on leave and accompanied her. Such was the secrecy that we parents weren't even told where the children were going. We found out from an official letter received a couple of days later that their destination was Torquay. Suddenly Becky and I were alone. It was very strange. The house had echoed to the sounds of the family, but now silence.

Then came the news that Bert was being transferred abroad. He had a short embarkation leave but didn't know where he was going. He was in the 50th Division and the rumours were that they were being sent to the Middle East. We were informed that he was 'on active service' with the Middle East Force. But we never knew where he was. At one time we had two letters which arrived almost simultaneously each containing a short cryptic message which meant nothing to us. In one he said 'Tell Ivy, sell your rabbits in August' and in the other 'So you rang Ivy's apartment? Did she agree about the rabbits?' Bernard solved the mystery. The initial letters of the last five words of the message in the first letter spelled out the name 'Syria' as did the initial letters of the first five words in the message in the second letter.

I was happy to return to the printing trade at Harrisons but I became disillusioned. The work was cheap commercial stuff where craftsmanship was not required. We were constantly being urged to 'get on with it' and cut out the frills. Matters came to a head in an altercation with the works manager. A director of the company was due to visit and the manager came around. I had a pile of paper on the feeding table. The manager approached me and shouted: 'Oi you,

Impressions of War

move that bloody lot!' I ignored him and he repeated the words. By this time all the other pressmen were listening. I turned to him and said: 'My name is Hodgson. You either call me that, or "pressman" but you don't address me as "Oi you."' He reddened but backed down. Later in private he apologised but the damage was done. I vowed to leave Harrisons at the first opportunity.

In summer 1941 we decided to visit the boys in Torquay. Bernard was writing regularly but we sensed that they were missing home and not entirely happy. We caught a night train that passed through Bristol. A German air raid had just finished when we arrived. Several engines and carriages just outside Bristol station were alight and there were palls of smoke about. We were hours late in arriving at Torquay. We decided that the two younger boys David and Ivor should return with us. They were ten and nine years old respectively and unhappy. Bernard, thirteen by this time, wanted to stay particularly as we had bought his bike down with us. He wanted to change his billet however and had found a spare place with a friend of his, but the lady couldn't take his brothers as well. With some misgivings we left him there. Later on he asked if he could come home for Christmas. Having returned he didn't want to go back. By this time he was fourteen and his future was beginning to occupy my mind. I remembered Bert's experience. You were too old at sixteen for an apprenticeship, he had been told. Both Becky and I thought that Bernard should leave school and be apprenticed. We discussed it with him and he agreed in principle but refused point blank to go into printing. He wanted a job where he didn't get his hands dirty.

The matter might have rested there and his schooling continued but for a chance remark by a neighbour. He told me that his company, a firm of builders, was finding it impossible to recruit boys of the right sort to train as surveyors. I told him about Bernard, an interview was arranged and a job was offered at £1 per week. That was the easy part. When we notified the school authorities it was a different matter. In those days there was no compulsion on parents to keep their children at school after the age of fourteen irrespective of the type of school attended. That didn't stop the authorities trying

A People at War

hard to change our minds. We resisted because we thought we were doing the right thing and Bernard himself was keen to start work.

The war continued but in 1942 things started to look far more hopeful. Later that year came the first good news we had had for some time. The Germans were being pushed back in the Western Desert in North Africa. We wondered where Bert was. We didn't know until his return that his division had become part of the famous Eighth Army – the Desert Rats – and he was in the thick of it.

In 1943, two years after joining Harrisons, I got the opportunity to leave. I wasn't sorry. My altercation with the manager had created an atmosphere that unsettled me. I couldn't be happy in a relatively large firm where the emphasis was on quantity rather than quality. After nearly twenty years of working where the standard of work was the thing that mattered, the cheap commercial attitude of firms like Harrisons was not for me. I joined a small press in Wembley owned by a Mr and Mrs Carradine. They were elderly and left the running of the firm to their son and daughter, Ron and Hazel. The press was named after the daughter and called the Hazell Press. Just after I joined, Ron was called up and Hazel ran it on her own. The work was commercial but there was some emphasis on quality, which suited me. Nearby was the Wembley Press, and for some time I was 'subbed out' to it, working three days per week at the Hazell and two days at the Wembley.

There was some comfort in the Hazell Press but little in the Wembley. It was a dump, owned by a rather miserable and unlikeable chap named Rose. The linotype room was so small that the machine took up all the space and the chap who worked it was sandwiched against the wall. I wondered how they got it in there in the first place and was told that it was delivered in pieces and installed on site. I say the Hazell Press was more comfortable but only because we had more space. There was little natural light and the toilet and washing facilities, typical in those days, were fairly primitive. There was no canteen of course and sandwiches were eaten squatting down by the machines. Yet I was happier there than I had been at Harrisons.

Impressions of War

While working at the Hazell Press in 1943 I got talking one day to another pressman who told me of a part-time job on the turnstiles at Wembley Stadium. It sounded interesting so I applied and was taken on. I didn't know how long it might last and never dreamt at the time that I would be doing it for eighteen years.

In June 1944 came the 'doodle-bugs' – the German V1 unmanned flying bomb. Lilian's career in the ATS had taken her to Scotland and Wales but now she was stationed on an anti-aircraft base at Whitley Bay on the East Coast. I said to Becky that little did we know in 1918 that there would be another war with Germany in our lifetime and that this time our children would be helping to defend us. By the end of 1944 we were experiencing some euphoria that the end of the war was in sight. The Allied landing on Normandy had taken place on 6 June, the Germans had been kicked out of Africa and Bert's letters home were decidedly more optimistic.

He told us in one letter of a few days leave in Alexandria in Egypt. On the Sunday evening he visited the Church Army canteen, signing the visitor's book on entering. Some twenty minutes later he heard a voice shouting: 'Who comes from Greenford?' It was a Royal Artillery sergeant named Richard Price who told Bert that he came from Southall, next to Greenford. 'Whereabouts do you live?' Bert was asked and replied: 'Well, the family now live in Wedmore Road but we lived in Rydal Crescent, Perivale before the war. The other pondered this and Bert's surname. 'You haven't got a sister named Lilian with a friend named Joan have you?' he asked. 'Yes' said Bert. 'And they both work at Sanderson's Wallpapers?' 'Yes' said Bert. 'Well' said Richard, 'I took your sister out a few times'. While Bert was getting his breath back Richard continued 'Do you remember calling out to your sister one night, at the back of the house, to come in?' 'Yes' said Bert. 'Well, I was the chap who was with her,' smiled Richard!

They were stationed near to each other and one evening Bert returned to his barracks to find Richard sitting on Bert's bed looking quite excited. His name had been pulled out of a hat to go on leave to England. He wrote down our new address in Wedmore Road and promised to visit us. By a remarkable coincidence, on the evening he

A People at War

arrived at our house not only was Lilian at home on leave but she opened the door to him! We were all bowled over with the excitement of his visit and hearing some first-hand news of Bert.

At Wedmore Road we had a good-size garden and I had to look after it. We were constantly being urged to 'dig for victory' so I concentrated on vegetable growing on the back half and with some success. The front half I laid to lawn and for the first time in my life I became the owner of a lawn mower.

A big difference between the Great War and the Second was radio. During the Great War people had to rely on newspapers, but now the news was brought right into their living rooms. The BBC employed war correspondents who gave first-hand accounts of battle areas. Radio also helped to keep up spirits with variety shows like 'Saturday Night Music Hall' and comedy programmes such as ITMA ('It's That Man Again') featuring comedian Tommy Handley.

Becky was out shopping one day when a package dropped from a passing lorry at her feet. The lorry didn't stop, so she brought the package home. We found it contained two dozen clockwork spiders. She took the lot to Greenford police station. The station sergeant was a little perplexed but said: 'You'd better leave them with us and come back in two weeks. If they are not claimed you can keep them.' As she left the police station she glanced back. The sergeant and two or three constables had taken out the contents of the package and the counter was alive with clockwork spiders! They were not claimed and Becky distributed them to young children.

At another time she lost her purse in Shepherds Bush market, just before Christmas. It contained about £5. The police didn't hold out much hope but a couple of days later she was asked to go to Greenford police station. The purse had been handed in at Shepherds Bush with its contents intact and sent over to Greenford. Becky asked for the name and address of the finder and was told: 'I wouldn't bother to write, it was only some bloody foreigner.' The name she was given seemed East European. She wrote giving thanks and enclosed a ten shilling note. She was tempted to take the reply she received up to Greenford police station and thrust it under the

Impressions of War

nose of the sergeant. The person who had written was not at all well off and was surprised at Becky's kindness.

I didn't visit Bernard Wetherall again during the war but we corresponded regularly. One day I got a letter from him to tell me that he had been booked to do a series of radio broadcasts about his life driving a bus in wartime. With his ready cockney wit he made them very funny and enjoyable.

In 1944 David became fourteen and we made the decision to take him out of school and get him apprenticed. David didn't mind a job where he got his hands dirty and he joined me at the Hazell Press as an apprentice compositor. Meanwhile Bernard was studying hard at night school three evenings a week following his career in building. Ivor, our youngest, was twelve.

David and I cycled to and from the Hazell Press together. One evening on our way home we heard the by now familiar drone of a doodlebug. Suddenly the noise stopped and we got off our bikes and flung ourselves to the ground. As it happened we were in no danger. The bomb hit the Glaxo factory in Greenford about a mile away.

We used to have lunch in a 'British Restaurant' near the Wembley Press. It was one of thousands set up by the Government during the war where you could get very simple basic meals for nine pence to a shilling. I remember cold spam, soggy and lumpy mashed potatoes and watery cabbage followed by apple pie (mostly pastry, little apple) covered with thin custard made from powdered milk and water. It was served cafeteria style and if you couldn't face the custard the server (usually a cheerful plump lady with an urchin haircut) would smile and call out: 'Pie in the nude is it?'

At last in 1945 the war came to an end. There were two celebrations: VE (Victory in Europe) in May and VJ (Victory over Japan) in August. Street parties were organised and the spirit of comradeship, so evident during the war, was never more marked. The utter relief that it was over could be seen on the faces of everyone.

I was overjoyed in 1945 when a Labour government came to power. At last the old order would be changed forever, I told myself. Now we had the opportunity to build a better Britain.

A People at War

At the end of the war Bernard Wetherall wrote a book *The Gardens of Paradise Alley* about our boyhood in Peckham.[58] It mentions Ted Smith and me and I read it with mounting nostalgia. In the copy he sent me Bernard had written: 'To my old mate Bert Hodgson who could laugh at anything.'

Street Party, Wedmore Road, Greenford, May 1945
On the middle (seated) row, David Hodgson is third from left (excluding child on lap) and Ivor Hodgson second from right

---

[58] The book was published in 1946 by Methuen in London.

6. Moving On

A corner of the Hazell Press had been rented out to a Mr Walter Phillips, who designed and marketed photographic mounts that the Press printed for him. He liked my work and insisted that I did his printing. Phillips told me one day that as soon as he could he would open his own press and ask me to work for him

Bert returned home in 1946 after four and a half years in the Middle East and North Africa, during which he had corresponded with a young lady in the WAAF (Women's Auxiliary Air Force). Her name was Ethel Stuart from Dungavel near Hamilton in Scotland. In true romantic fashion she and Bert arranged to meet under the clock at King's Cross station. Four words were exchanged: 'I'm Ethel'. 'I'm Bert.' They fell in love and were married in 1947 in the private chapel on the Duke of Hamilton's estate at Dungavel where Ethel had been brought up. Becky, Lilian, Bert and I made the journey.

Bert was anxious to get back to work in print, His pre-war printing experience had been very limited and after joining David and me at the Hazell Press he enrolled at evening classes. Lilian returned to her pre-war job at Sandersons in Perivale. Richard Price, the Royal Artillery sergeant whom Bert had met in Alexandria and who visited us while on leave, had also returned to the firm. They fell in love and married in Greenford also in 1947. Richard became known as 'Jack' in the family.

Walter Phillips' plans saw fulfilment in 1947 when the Unicorn Press was opened in Perivale and became a commercial success. Phillips wanted a quality product and the work was very exacting but I was doing something I enjoyed. One of the members of the Press was Phillips' brother-in-law Frank Thornwell, a charming man with a dreadful stutter. He could make fun of it however. He had been in the thick of things during the Blitz on London. Once when crawling through the rubble of a building he put up a temporary prop. As he

Moving On

progressed he heard someone up above say: 'Take that prop out of there, I need it here.' Thornwell shouted out: 'Leave it alone!' 'If I'd stuttered then' he went on 'I wouldn't be here telling the story now!'

Wedding of Lilian Hodgson and Richard Price, 26 July 1947

Left to right: Joan Lodge, Glyn Rees (best man), Mary Morris née Price (sister), Richard, Lilian, Herbert Hodgson, Rebecca Hodgson, Ethel Hodgson (Bert's wife)

The excitement of that year was tempered by Becky becoming ill. After a number of visits to the hospital she was diagnosed as having cancer. It was shattering news. An operation was scheduled for January 1948 and on the surgeon's advice I applied for Bernard to be sent home on compassionate leave. By the time he arrived home the operation had been successfully carried out. My sisters Lily and Kate helped out by staying with us and nursing Becky.

After a month at home, Bernard was sent back to Palestine. Disembarking from the troopship in Egypt he was put on a train to Haifa. Going through Gaza the train was blown up by a Jewish terrorist organisation. Thirteen servicemen were killed and many more seriously injured, but Bernard escaped with minor injuries.

Impressions of War

In May Becky suffered a relapse and entered hospital for another operation. The surgeon warned me to prepare for the worst and once again Bernard found himself on a plane flying back to the UK. Becky again pulled through, came home and was nursed back to health by my sisters. It was a traumatic time for everybody but poor Becky suffered terribly.

Bernard left the army in August. He had married Joan, a Greenford girl and they had a lovely daughter Valerie, our first grandchild. In 1949 it was David's turn to be called up. He went into the Royal Corps of Signals, hated every minute of it and was glad to be demobbed two years later. Meanwhile Ivor had left school in 1947 and taken a job in a boot and shoe repair shop in Greenford. Like Bernard he didn't want to enter the printing trade.

Robert Maynard wanted to re-open the Raven Press but I had to tell him that in all fairness to Walter Philips I couldn't leave the Unicorn Press. It was still a new business and Phillips relied too much on me and others. Maynard accepted this and we remained on good terms and in touch with each other until his death in 1966.

Herbert Hodgson and Bernard Wetherall in 1947

Moving On

In 1950 a letter arrived from our landlords, offering to sell us the house for £1000. Like our parents, we had always lived in rented accommodation. Buying a house had never been a serious consideration. At fifty-seven I took out my first mortgage.

The country was desperately short of houses. Lilian and Jack occupied two rooms in our house for the first few years of their marriage, while Bert and Ethel rented rooms elsewhere. Food, clothing, furniture, coal, petrol, building materials and confectionery were rationed. There was talk about the country being on its knees.

Then in 1951 the unthinkable happened; the Conservative Party won the General Election. The Labour Party forecast a return to the dole queues of the 1920s and 30s and I believed it. It didn't happen and I began to realise that the old order had changed. I was glad that we had fought, through the trade union movement, the battles of the first part of the century but I now became irked at some of the things which were being said and done in the name of trade unionism. I think too that my children were having some influence on me. As the decade progressed my loyalty to the Labour Party was unswerving but I became more critical of it.

We had thought that the 1920s and 30s were decades of change but the 1950s eclipsed them. The biggest event was the coming of television. I had seen one in a shop window in 1938 but now they were appearing in people's houses. That all programmes were in black and white only and that the maximum screen size was nine inches did not detract one bit from the wonder of this new medium of current affairs and entertainment.

Before the war only rich and middle-class people owned cars. Now second-hand pre-war cars could be afforded by all and sundry. The shops started filling up with all sorts of consumer products and rationing finally came to an end. Electrical goods of every kind, many of which had never been seen before, were on display. Becky was amazed that Bernard and Joan's Hoover washing machine was able to get rid of the printing ink stains in my working shirts. Old-fashioned lino gave way to fitted carpets, instant coffee was introduced, electric radios were in all the shops and electric record players replaced radiograms. Long-playing records appeared –

Impressions of War

marvellously light in weight compared with the old 78s and giving six times the length of playing time.

I still played the banjo and piano indoors for my own amusement but Bert and Bernard were now the musicians in the family. Bert is in great demand playing sax in local dance bands. Bernard plays the trumpet and his love is for New Orleans jazz. He and fellow enthusiasts play in a band in Crawley in West Sussex.

No sooner had David left the army that it was Ivor's turn to go in the forces but he opted for the RAF. After two years, during which he had some training in communications on teleprinters he joined the Shell Company and remained with them.

In 1951 Lilian presented us with our first grandson Gareth (Gary). Needing more room she and Jack bought their first house in South Ruislip. David introduced us to Doreen, a Greenford girl. They became engaged and were married in Greenford in 1952, moving in with Becky and me. In 1953 Ethel and Bert, who had already bought their first house in Greenford, announced a forthcoming event and little Elaine duly arrived. The whole family would gather at our house on Christmas evening and we'd celebrate together. It seemed everybody was happy but of course nothing lasts forever.

Tragedy struck when Becky had a recurrence of cancer. There was nothing more that surgery could do. My sisters Lily and Kate moved in to nurse her. In January 1956 she died aged 60.

Her death was the most shattering experience I could imagine. We had known each other for 41 years and had been married for 37. She was the finest wife any man could have and the finest mother to our children. She looked after us all and made many sacrifices for us. The way in which the children have grown up is to her credit and perhaps her finest testimonial.

In 1958 I had to face my impending retirement. When I discussed it with Walter Phillips he asked what I wanted to do and I told him I'd rather go on working. He smiled. 'I was hoping you might say that. Look, none of us wants you to go. You can carry on as long as you like'. We shook hands. It was the best thing he could have said.

Also in 1958 I had a visit from Bernard Wetherall who had bought with him some fascinating mementoes he'd discovered: the

Moving On

two letters I'd written to him from France[1] and a letter written to him by our old Headmaster Mr Chase in 1915.

In 1958 Ivor introduced me to Kathy, a Hampshire girl and they were married in Greenford in late December that year. The last of my children had taken the plunge. Like Lilian/Jack and David/Doreen they lived at Wedmore Road at the start of their marriage before buying their first house in Ruislip Gardens. For the first time I was alone in the house. It all seemed strangely quiet. I had a telephone installed and family contact was easy.

For some years my sisters Lily and Kate had been living together in Kate's house in Erith, Kent in a house bequeathed to her by her husband. Kate had married in 1941 after nursing an old friend through her final illness and had then married the bereaved husband Ernest Elderfield. She contracted cancer in the early 1960s but after her death in 1965 the house passed to her stepson. I suggested that Lily should come and live with me and she readily accepted.

In 1961 Bernard and Joan spent a holiday in North Wales and visited the National Library in Aberystwyth, After Bernard explained who he was the cases containing Gregynog books were opened for him to see my name in the books. Then he was told: 'There is someone here we would like you to meet'. It was Idris Jones, my old colleague from Gregynog, who for some years had worked at the library.[2] Bernard had a cine camera with him and he and Idris were filmed together. Seeing Idris again was quite a surprise for me.

I was never a regular cinema-goer but I felt I should see *Lawrence of Arabia* when it was released in 1963. A brilliant and absorbing film was spoilt for me by the choice of Peter O'Toole in the lead role. He is far too tall. Lawrence commanded attention with his piercing blue eyes rather than through the physical presence

---

[1] Reproduced in chapter two above.

[2] The Gregynog Press closed in 1940. In 1954 most of its machinery was taken to the National Library of Wales. In 1963 Gregynog Hall was donated to the University of Wales. The University reopened the press under the title Gwasg Gregynog in 1978 and it became a charity in 2002. The press printed the first documents for the new Welsh National Assembly in 1999.

Impressions of War

portrayed by O'Toole. This is not a criticism of the actor's performance, which was very good, but all the way through the film I kept thinking: 'You are not Lawrence.'

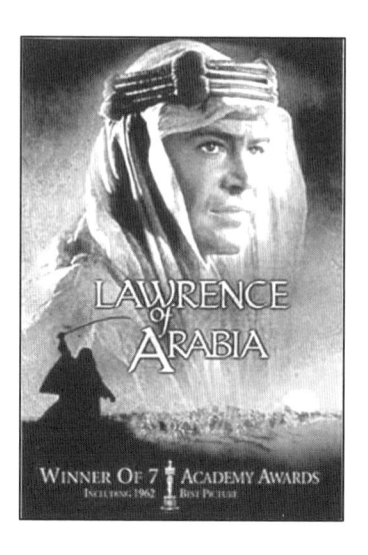

Poster for the 1962 Film *Lawrence of Arabia*

In 1963 at 70 years of age I felt I should retire. Walter Phillips repeated what he had said before: 'You can stay as long as you like, Bert'. I was given handsome presents, a cheque from the management and an inscribed pewter tankard from the staff. What mixed feelings I had as I cycled home!

I needed something to do and, frankly, a little more money than my State and Union pensions amounted to. I found a part-time job in a car showroom washing and valeting cars. The work was outside and the winter took its toll on my health. I had a severe bout of bronchitis and the doctor advised me against working outside. In addition he counselled me to give up smoking which (after fifty six years) I succeeded in doing.

My sister Lily had suffered from arthritis for many years and as her condition worsened she required increasing nursing care. She had

Moving On

never married and had spent her life in service and the care of others. She had been a dedicated Salvation Army member and then served in the St John Ambulance Brigade. Now she herself was in need of constant care and so she entered a nursing home in Southall. She died peacefully in 1970.

I got another part-time job, this time in a bakery cleaning utensils. I developed a rash which my doctor ascribed to the pastry in the bakery and so I decided to give in my notice. I was amazed that in the 1960s I had found a sweatshop like that bakery. After all the battles which had been fought by trades unions over the years to improve conditions here was a workplace which was a throwback to the turn of the century. I remembered the bakeries in my boyhood where men worked a 100 hours per week in stifling conditions. This bakery was little better. I could not stand aside and see men exploited like that and urged them to join a trade union. On the day when I was about to offer my resignation I was approached by the manager who asked: 'What the bloody hell do think you're doing and who the bloody hell do you think you are?' I told him that the conditions in the bakery were a disgrace and he called me 'a bloody Communist'. Before he could sack me I walked out.

That experience made me decide to write these memoirs. Many people through the years have been interested in my stories of my boyhood, the Great War, my meetings with Lawrence of Arabia, the printing of his book, my time in Wales and the Gregynog Press and so on. Now I had another story to add to all the others. After quitting the bakery I needed something to do, and so I took up pen and paper.

Then I had a slight scare about my health. Sitting down one morning I realised that I couldn't get up from my chair. I felt dazed and couldn't move my left arm. When the doctor arrived he gave me a thorough examination. My mouth was crooked, I had a funny feeling in my arm and I couldn't clench my hand. He told me I'd had a slight stroke and there was no need to worry: to get the feeling back in my hand and arm I should pound the piano. I did and it worked.

I had some financial worries and my family advised me to sell the house. I wanted to find a small flat. One night we were discussing the matter and Ethel read out an advertisement in the local paper. An

Impressions of War

elderly widower wished to share his maisonette with another elderly widower. The address was just around the corner from us. We phoned and went round. Bill Rhodes and I hit it off right away and said we would 'give each other a try'. I moved in. Not only were my financial worries eased but I found Bill to be a charming companion.

I sorted out the personal belongings I wanted to keep and hesitated over the contents of my tin trunk. Amongst other things were seventeen Gregynog books that I had purchased as they were printed. I had treasured them for many years. Now I had to decide what to do with them. I asked the family. The answer was unanimous, sell them and spend the money on yourself.

When Bernard approached Sotheby's in New Bond Street he was introduced to their book expert. Bernard said: 'My father has some Gregynog books to sell'. The man smiled and said: 'Well I know that you're genuine, you pronounced Gregynog correctly!' The books were duly entered at auction and all but one was sold. They fetched in excess of £2500. With that in the bank as well as the house sale my financial situation was now secure.

I have managed to keep in fairly good health although for a couple of years I did have an attack of shingles on my face. My doctor ascribed this to a weakness in my nerve ends caused over fifty years before by shell-shock in France![3]

It is four delightful years since I moved in with Bill Rhodes. I am sure Bill feels the same. He had lost his wife before he met me and without realising it we both needed the company and friendship. Our tastes in food and entertainment and our senses of humour coincide exactly. It seems that we both have the temperament necessary for a successful and convivial friendship. I cannot recall one cross word spoken in the four years.

---

[3] Sometime in the 1970s, Herbert's son Ivor was chatting with his colleagues in his office about the First World War. Ron Keyworth spoke: 'An uncle of mine got the VC in the war.' Ivor butted in: 'Yes, Corporal Keyworth,' and Ron asked: 'How did you know he was a Corporal?' Ivor replied: 'I grew up hearing about him from my Dad, who was in the same battalion.' Everyone was amazed at what a small world it is.

Moving On

Herbert Hodgson with his Sons on his 80th Birthday, 2 June 1973

Left to right: Bert, Ivor, Bernard, Herbert, David

Recently we spent a few days at a home for the elderly in Trowbridge, Wiltshire. One day some visitors, a middle-aged married couple, arrived and they seemed interested in my stories so much so that we were invited to lunch at their lovely home the following day. When the main course was served both Bill and I failed to recognise the meat and asked politely what it was. 'Pheasant' we were told, and it came from Harrods. A few days later, when it was his turn to do a little shopping from our local grocery store, Bill said: 'I'm just off to Harrods to get the pheasant!'

My father died on Saturday 10th August 1974. He was 81 years of age. The day before I called in to see him at the maisonette he shared with Bill Rhodes. I was to go on holiday the next day and I wanted to say goodbye for a couple of weeks. I arrived about four in the afternoon and he was in good spirits. We chatted about various matters. Just before six he said: 'I'm feeling rather tired Bern, I'll just have a little lie down. You go if you like, thanks for coming'. With that he went into his bedroom. I waited a while and then peeped in. He was lying on his back on his bed, breathing heavily but not in a laboured way. After another ten minutes I looked in again to see him lying in the same position. He seemed unlikely to wake up soon, so I decided to leave. When I got home I called Bert and Ethel and told them of my visit. In the morning Bill Rhodes came and asked them to come to the maisonette. Dad was still lying on his bed. He had not woken up from the sleep in which I had left him.

Bernard Hodgson

2008 Gregynog Festival – Books Printed by Herbert Hodgson

Controller David Vickers (left) and Bernard Hodgson (right) with his daughters Gillian Smith (left) and Elizabeth Hall (right)

Index

Abbeville, 37, 40, 58
Abercrombie, Lascelles, 97
Aberystwyth, 85, 88, 129
Africa, 119, 120, 124
Albany Road Mission, 4-5, 11
Albert (town), 37, 54, 58
Albion press, 66, 76, 79, 87
Andrew, Evelyn (Dolly), 93
apprenticeship, 14-15, 30, 102, 105, 107, 118, 122
Arab Revolt, 67, 69, 72, 77, 81
Ashendene Press, 64, 84

Baden-Powell, Robert, 19
Badger, Mr, 92-3
Badrick, Alice, 109
Bairnsfather, Bruce, 53
Ballantyne, R. M., 18
Barclamb, Bill, 46
Barnett, Henrietta, 11
Barter, Major-General Charles, 54
Battalion, 24th London, 32, 39
BBC, 23, 108, 121
Belgium, 37, 58, 113
Bennett, Billy, 108
Bermondsey, 1, 28, 99, 114
Béthune, 37, 44
Bettws Cedewain, 84, 89-6, 99, 102-3, 111-12
Blackfriars, 17-18, 24-27, 62, 64, 89
Blitz, 26, 124
Boer War, 6, 19, 31, 35, 50
Boult, Sir Adrian, 97
Bowen, Florrie, 93
Bray, Horace, 87-8, 97, 101, 106-7
Brighton, 21-2, 63
Britain, Battle of, 114
Brough Superior motorcycle, 76, 101
Bumpus booksellers, 83-4, 99, 101
Burge, Bella and Dick, 26

Carency, 37, 55
Carradine, Hazel, 119
Carradine, Ron, 119
Chamberlain, Neville, 111
Chappell of Bond Street, 24
Chase, Mr, 6, 14, 129
Cherry, Bob, 19
Chiswick, 65, 72
Church Lads' Brigade, 20, 27, 31
Churchill, Winston, 82, 114
Conservative Party, 96, 108, 114, 127
Cook, Richard Llewellyn, 59-60
Cordon, Lou, 114
Crawley, 22, 128
Cuinchy, Battle of, 44, 45
Cutler, Desmond, 113

D Day, 120
Davies, David, 86
Davies, Gwendoline, 86-7, 94, 97, 99, 102-3
Davies, Margaret, 86-7, 94, 97
Davies, Sir Walford, 97

Ealing, 110, 117
Edward VIII's abdication, 109
Egypt, 77, 120, 125
Eisteddfods, 94, 96
Elderfield, Ernest, 129
Elephant and Castle, 14, 107
Elliot, G. H., 23
Étaples, 37, 59
Eu, 37, 58
evacuation of children, 117
Evans, Ethel, 94

Farnborough, 19, 20
Faulkner, Keith, 97
Festubert, Battle of, 35-6, 45
Figg, Captain Donald, DSO, 39-40

135

Impressions of War

Fisher, George, 87, 101, 104
Flynn, John, 7
Forster, E. M., 77

Gaza, 125
General Strike of 1926, 82
George V, King, 39
German offensives of 1918, 57-9
Givenchy, Battle of, 38-40, 48
Golden Cockerel Press, 84
Gravenstafel Ridge, 59
Graves, Robert, 45, 81
Greenford, 111, 113, 117, 120-9
Gregynog Hall, 85-7, 90, 94, 97, 129
Gregynog Press, 84-91, 97, 99, 101, 103-7, 109, 112, 129, 131-2
Gurkas, 34

Haberly, Loyd, 101
Haig, General Douglas, 59
Hall, Elizabeth, née Hodgson, 134
Hall, Henry, 108
Handley, Tommy, 108, 121
Hardie, James Keir, 27
Hardy, Thomas, 77
Harrisons, 117-19
Harrop, Dorothy A., 104-5
Harrow Weald, 97, 106
Hatch End, 107-8
Hazell Press, 119-24
Hellfire Corner, 51
Henry, Ernest, 113
Hermes, Gertrude, 72, 101, 107
High Wood, Battle of, 45, 54
Hill, Reverend Rowland, 26
Hind, Arthur, 93-4, 103
Hind, Mr and Mrs Daniel, 90-3
Hodge, John, 64
Hodgson, Bernard, 89, 91, 95, 99, 105, 107, 111, 113, 117-19, 122, 125-9, 132-4
Hodgson, Bert, 62, 91-6, 99, 102, 107, 110-12, 117-21, 124-5, 127-8, 133-4

Hodgson, David, 97-9, 107, 117-18, 122-9, 133
Hodgson, Doreen (née Miller), 128-9
Hodgson, Dorothy (Dolly), 1-2
Hodgson, Elaine, 128
Hodgson, Elizabeth (Lily), 2, 14-15, 22, 125, 128-30
Hodgson, Elizabeth Jane, née Skidmore, 1-14, 18, 24, 48, 84
Hodgson, Elsie, 2, 14-15, 99, 115
Hodgson, Ethel, née Stuart, 124-5, 127-8, 131, 134
Hodgson, Ivor, 99, 110, 117-18, 123, 126, 128-9, 132, 133
Hodgson, Joan (née Rainton), 126-7
Hodgson, John George, 1-6, 9-18, 24, 30, 48, 63, 84, 108
Hodgson, Kate, 2, 14-15, 125, 128-9
Hodgson, Kathy (née Gunner), 129
Hodgson, Lilian, 62, 91-4, 102, 107, 112, 114, 120-1, 124-5, 127-9
Hodgson, Rebecca. *See* Moore, Rebecca
Hodgson, Valerie, 126
Hornby, C. H. St John, 64
Hughes-Stanton, Blair, 72, 101, 104-6
Hylton, Jack, 108

Indian Corps, British, 35

John, Augustus, 72
Johnson, Anthony Rolfe, 97
Johnson, Jack, 42
Jones, Dai, 93, 94, 96, 103
Jones, Dr Thomas, 87, 88, 104
Jones, Hywel, 93-4, 96
Jones, Idris, 87, 101, 112, 129
Jones, Jack, 94-5
Jones, John, 87, 101

Kelmscott Press, 84
Kemmel, 37, 58-9
Kennington, 32, 56

Index

Kennington, Eric, 72, 74
Kensington, 18, 100
Keyworth, Lance-Corporal Leonard, VC, 39-40, 132
Keyworth, Ron, 132
Kipling, Rudyard, 50, 77

La Bassée, 36, 44-5
Labour Party, 27, 108, 122, 127
Lauder, Harry, 23
Lawrence of Arabia. *See* Lawrence, T. E.
Lawrence of Arabia (film), 129-30
Lawrence, T. E., 45, 67-83, 100-1, 104-5, 129-31
Lewis, Gwendoline Kate, 65, 69, 100
Lewis, May, 94-6
Lodge, Joan, 120, 125
London Infantry Division, 47th, 39, 54
London School of Printing, 17, 67
Loos, Battle of, 45, 50
Lorraine, Violet, 53
Lys, German Offensive 1918, 57-9

Mallock Gee, Walter, 20
Manning Pike, Jane, 100
Manning Pike, Mary, 100
Manning Pike, Roy, 65-76, 79-83, 88-9, 100-1, 105
Mason, John, 101
Maude, Alan H., 39
Maynard, Robert, 84-88, 97, 101-2, 104, 106-7, 109, 112, 126
McCance, William, 98, 101
Meddings, Reggie, 96
Menin Road, 51
Messines, Battle of, 59-60
Middle East, 77, 117, 124
Moore, Alan, 98
Moore, Elizabeth (Li), 99, 107, 114
Moore, Rebecca (Becky Hodgson), 27-9, 34, 48, 52-3, 56-7, 62, 84-5,

89-2, 99, 107, 110-14, 117-18, 120-8
Morris, Mary, née Price, 125

Nash, Paul, 72
Neuve Chapelle, Battle of, 34-5
New Zealand Expeditionary Force, 59-60
Newtown, 84-5, 89- 96, 99, 101
Normandy, 120

O'Leary, Michael, VC, 44
O'Toole, Peter, 129-30
Otago Regiment, New Zealand Expeditionary Force, 59, 60
Ottoman Empire, 77
Owen, Robert, 93

Paddington, 64, 75, 77, 85, 87
Palestine, 125
Parker, Agnes Miller, 98, 101, 107, 109
Passchendaele, Battle of, 37, 57
Passingham, Ian, 58, 60
Payne, Jack, 108
Pearce, Percy, 48
Pearce, Tom, 48
Peckham, 6, 14, 17-20, 62, 69, 72, 76, 123
Perivale, 110-13, 120, 124
Péronne, 37, 54
Phillips, Walter 124, 126, 128, 130
Pinner, 106-8, 110
Polygon Wood, 59
Price, Gareth (Gary), 128
Price, Richard (Jack), 120, 124-5, 127-9
Pulteney, Lieutenant-General Sir William Pulteney, 54

Raven Press, 107, 109-12, 116, 126
Rees, Glyn, 125
Rhodes, Bill, 132-4
Robey, George, 53

137

Impressions of War

Rouse, Alfred, 35, 98
Royal Air Force, 67, 102, 112, 114, 128
Royal Flying Corps, 34-5
Royal Irish Fusiliers, 9th Battalion, 57-60
Royal West Surrey Regiment, 32-8
Ruislip, 128-9
Russia, 57, 109

Sassoon, Siegfried, 77
Scouting for Boys, 19
Seraucourt-le-Grand, 58
Seven Pillars of Wisdom, 65-84, 87-8, 99, 104-5
Sevenoaks, 19, 43
Shackleton, Sir Ernest, 25
Shaw, George Bernard, 77, 82, 97
Shrapnel Corner, 51
Sims, Harry, 115
Sims, Jimmy, 115
Sims, Stanley, 115
Smith, Gillian, née Hodgson, 134
Smith, Ted, 19, 21, 24, 31-2, 34, 37, 46-8, 63, 123
socialism, 11, 27, 93, 114
Somme, Battle of the, 37, 40, 53-8
Somme, German Offensive 1918, 57
Southall, 120, 131
Southampton, 34, 52, 60
Southwark, 56, 64
St Albans, 33-4, 39
St Quentin, 37, 58
St Quentin-la-Motte, 37, 58
Stratton, Eugene, 23
strikes, 60, 61, 63, 82
Suddaby, Elsie, 97
Surrey Chapel, the, 26

Tarri, Suzette, 108
Territorial Army, 8, 30-2
Thames, River, 8, 65, 76
Thomas Tilling Ltd, 18
Thornwell, Frank, 124, 125

Tilley, Vesta, 23
Torquay, 117-18
trade unions, 61-5, 69, 71, 84, 89, 101, 117, 127, 131
Trades Union Congress, 82
Tregascus, Hugh, 109
Tregynon, 84-6, 89, 91, 94, 112
Trinder, Tommy, 108
Turks, 67-70, 77

Unicorn Press, 124, 126
USA, 60, 63, 65, 74, 100

Valerie, Hodgson, 126
Venetian Dance Band, 94-5
Vickers, David, 105, 134
Victoria platen printing press, 16, 66, 87

W. H. Smith, 64, 102
Walworth Road, 2, 27, 91
Waterloo Station, 32, 52
Waters, Doris, 108
Waters, Elsie, 108
Wedmore Road, 113, 115, 120-1, 123, 129
Wembley Press, 119, 122
Wetherall, Bernard, 7, 19-21, 23, 27-31, 34, 46-48, 52, 63, 89, 113, 122-3, 126, 128
Wetherall, Marie, 29, 48, 63, 113
Wharton, Harry, 19
Williams, Dai, 93, 103
Williams, Mabel, 94-5
Wilson, J. G., 83-4, 99-102
Wilson, Jeremy, 77, 81
Winchester, 56, 60
Wood, Peter, 65, 101
Woodgate, Mr, 19, 20, 43-4
Wulverghem, 58-60

Ypres, 37, 58-9
Ypres Salient, 51, 58-60